THE PLA NAVY

CHINESE MILITARY LIBRARY

The PLA Navy

Gao Xiaoxing
Weng Saifei
Zhou Dehua
Sun Yanhong
Chen Liangwu
Chen Gang

Original edition copyright ©2012 China Intercontinental Press
CN Times Books edition copyright ©2014 by CN Times Books, Inc.

CN Times Books is grateful to China Intercontinental Press for granting the exclusive right to publish this book in the English language in North America.

All rights reserved. No part of this publication may be reproduced, distributed, or transmitted in any form or by any means, including photocopying, recording, or other electronic or mechanical methods, without the prior written permission of the publisher, except in the case of brief quotations embodied in critical reviews and certain other noncommercial uses permitted by copyright law. For permission requests, write to the publisher, addressed "Attention: Permissions Coordinator," at the address below.

BEIJING MEDIATIME BOOKS CO., LTD.
CN Times Books, Inc.
501 Fifth Avenue
New York, NY 10017
cntimesbooks.com

ORDERING INFORMATION
Quantity sales: Special discounts are available on quantity purchases by corporations, associations, and others. For details, contact the publisher at the address above. **Orders by U.S. trade bookstores and wholesalers:** Please contact Ingram Publisher Services: Tel: (866) 400-5351; Fax: (800) 838-1149; or customer.service@ingrampublisherservices.com.

ISBN 978-1-62774-023-4

Printed in the United States of America

CONTENTS

Preface • vii
Introduction • iv
Abbreviations • xiii

1. An Arduous Birth from the Flames of War • 1
Naval Command Born in a Small Village • 2
"Number 1 Announcement" • 6
Trial by Fire • 12

2. Fierce Battles in Southeast Coastal Areas • 19
Breaking through the Blockade: Naval Campaign near East Zhejiang Province • 26
The August Sixth Sea Battle • 40

3. Safeguarding Sovereignty over the South China Sea • 47
Air Battles above Hainan Island • 48
Battle of the Paracel Islands • 59

4. From Yellow to Blue Waters • 71
"An Expo of Various Outdated Vessels" • 71
The Development of the People's Navy • 73
Sailing the Oceans • 85

5. Establishment of the PLAN • 89
PLAN Headquarters • 89
The PLAN's Three Fleets • 90
Five Branches of the PLAN • 92

6. The PLAN's Main Weaponry and Equipment • 105
Naval Vessels • 105
Submarines • 119
Naval Aircraft • 124
Marine Corps Weapons • 130
Coastal Defense Unit Weapons • 131

7. Doing Multiple Military Tasks • 133
Escort • 133
International Humanitarian Rescue • 150
Disaster Relief in China • 155
National Defense Scientific Research • 162

8. The Course of Friendship • 175
China's Warships Abroad • 176
Port Calls by Foreign Navies • 187
Joint Military Exercises • 192
The Chinese Naval Cadets Week International • 200
A Naval Carnival in Qingdao • 202

Bibliography • 213

PREFACE

SINCE THE START of the twenty-first century, with the rise of China's overall national and military strength, China's defense policies, military strategy and military development have increasingly become the focus of the world's attention, and many books have been published abroad of late about China's army, the People's Liberation Army (PLA). Unfortunately, though, due to a lack of firsthand information on which to base some of the books, the accuracy of their content is debatable.

What kind of an army is the PLA? At what stages of development are the various branches of the Chinese armed forces? What levels of development have China's military weapons and equipment reached?

Such questions are of great concern to the international community and are spurring lively discussions among the media abroad. For this reason, we believe that publishing a vivid and accurate series of books on the Chinese army, for both domestic and foreign readers, is pertinent.

There are three books in the first series on the Chinese Army, namely: *The People's Liberation Army*, *The PLA Navy* and *The PLA Air Force*. The second series of three will deal with *The PLA Aviation Corps*, *The PLA Marines* and *The PLA Airborne Force*. The third series will be presented in four volumes: *The Chinese Maritime Escortion*, *Chinese Peacekeepers Overseas*, *The Chinese Army and International Security Cooperation* and *The Chinese Army and Humanitarian Relief*. Each volume will contain from 50,000 to 100,000 words, and there will be hundreds of valuable photos. The three series constitute an effort to focus on the history of the Chinese armed forces, their current circumstances and their future growth and development by way of many interesting examples and details, to show the overall face of the People's Liberation Army from multiple angles.

Throughout the process of planning and writing the series, we invited experts from PLA-related departments, military academies and research institutions to participate, to ensure the authority and accuracy of the content. This series has also had the strong support and guidance of the Information Office of China's Ministry of National Defense. We believe, in fact, that the active participation of the military in this project has made the series far more in-depth than it might otherwise have been.

Due to the knowledge limitations of the editor, in the process of attempting to reflect this great theme of the Chinese People's Liberation Army, inevitably there will be errata and deficiencies. Readers' criticisms and corrections on these points are welcome.

Editor
January 2012

INTRODUCTION

ON APRIL 23, 1949, the first naval force of the Chinese People's Liberation Army Navy (Chinese Navy, or People's Navy, for short), the East China Military Area Navy, was established at Baima Temple in Taizhou, Jiangsu Province. The newly established force faced the arduous tasks of reconstructing deserted ports and rebuilding bomb-damaged shipyards and quays. The Navy's only warships and vessels, the majority of which had been built before or during the Second World War by the United States, the United Kingdom, Japan and other countries, had all been acquired through surrender, confiscation or requisition during battle. The performance of these out-of-date naval vessels lagged behind that of newer warships.

In February 1953, Chairman Mao boarded the People's Navy warship *Changjiang* for an inspection. After staying with the sailors for four days and three nights, he wrote, "We must establish a powerful naval force to fight imperialist aggression."

At that time, despite extremely tight defense spending, the Chinese government allocated large sums for the People's Navy and purchased four destroyers from the Soviet Union. In 1954, the first two of these were delivered and put into service. Thus, the first destroyer fleet of the People's Navy was established. One year later, vessels and warships of the People's Navy joined the battle array in Army, Navy and Air Force joint maneuvers on the Liaodong Peninsula.

On January 18, 1955, five landing transport fleets comprising 142 warships and other vessels, and combat formations comprising 46 frigates, gunboats and escort boats, conquered the Yijiangshan Islands in coordination with the Army and the Air Force. That was the first time the PLA conducted a successful sea-crossing-landing operation in cooperation with the other branches.

Since then, the People's Navy has won many victories in battles to defend China's coastal areas, to counter the harassment of the KMT Navy and to defend against foreign troop invasions. In fact, in the more than 60 years since it was born, the People's Navy has engaged in combat more than 1,200 times and killed more than 7,000 enemies. More than 400 enemy vessels and warships have been captured, damaged or sunk, and more than 500 enemy aircraft have been shot down or damaged.

In the 1970s, military revolutions were raging around the world. In the summer of 1979, the former Chinese leader Deng Xiaoping, now back in power, boarded the home-built missile destroyer, the Jinan, to inspect it as an element of coastal defense. He said to the admirals around him, "The ocean is not a narrow city moat, and the Navy should not be defenders of a city. To establish and build a strong and wealthy China, we should head out to the world and face the ocean." Since then, the routes of the vessels of the People's Navy have expanded from sailing along China's coastline to sailing the oceans.

In May 1980, a fleet of several warships flying "August 1" army flags set sail from Shanghai. They passed through Balintang Channel on their way to the Pacific. The warships were providing security for the launching of long-range carrier rockets to designated areas in the South Pacific Ocean. This was the first time that surface ships of the People's Navy sailed beyond China's territorial waters and out into the ocean.

Since that first move, the People's Navy has made strides, and its routes have expanded to include the oceans. In May 1983, PLAN warships and vessels arrived at the Zengmu Reef, at the southernmost tip of China. From 1984 to 1985, PLAN sailed across the boundless Pacific and made a long voyage to the South Pole. In 1985, a naval warship formation paid a first visit to the Indian Ocean.

In 1989, the first Chinese naval training ship *Zhenghe* crossed the

International Date Line and sailed into the West Pacific Ocean, on what was the Navy's first visit to Hawaii.

But December 26, 2008, has gone down in history as a turning point for the People's Navy. The Chinese Naval Escort Force, comprising the *Wuhan* and *Haikou* missile destroyers and the comprehensive depot ship *Weishanhu*, set sail for the Gulf of Aden and Somalia that day to do escort work. And so China's naval warships had sailed into a new era.

China's naval equipment has improved rapidly, thanks to the great achievements resulting from the implementation of reform and the opening up policy. Today, Chinese warships and vessels perform convoy tasks in Somalia waters off Africa, far away from China's territorial waters, and they cruise in the South China Sea. In addition, Chinese naval personnel have done painstaking work to establish the first scientific investigation station at the South Pole and an oceanographic station on Yongshu Reef in the Spratly Islands. The routes of China's naval forces now take them to goodwill visits all over the world, to seven continents and across four oceans.

A powerful Chinese naval force will be a strong safeguard to world peace. It will bring the sincerity and friendship of the Chinese people to the world and promote a bright future of peaceful cooperation and mutual development, just as the famous Chinese mariner Zheng He and his fleet did over 600 years ago.

ABBREVIATIONS

ASCM	Anti-Ship Cruise Missile
CPC	Communist Party of China
CCCPC	Central Committee of the Communist Party of China
CMC	Central Military Commission
DDG	Guided-missile destroyer
ESF	East Sea Fleet
EW	Electronic warfare
EUNAVFOR	European Union Naval Force
FFG	Guided-missile frigate
GSD	General Staff Department
HY	Hai Ying ("Sea Hawk")
KMT	Kuomintang (Chinese Nationalist Party)
MR	Military Region
NSF	North Sea Fleet
PLA	People's Liberation Army
PLAAF	People's Liberation Army Air Force
PLAN	People's Liberation Army Navy
PLANAF	People's Liberation Army Navy Air Force
PRC	People's Republic of China
PT-boat	Patrol Torpedo Boat
SAM	Surface-to-air-missile

SSF	South Sea Fleet
SU	Sukhoi aircraft
SVN	South Vietnamese Navy
SY	Shang You ("Upstream")
UAV	Unmanned Air Vehicles
UNESCO	United Nations Educational, Scientific and Cultural Organization
USN	U.S. Navy
YG	Ying Ji ("Eagle Strike")

CHAPTER 1

An Arduous Birth from the Flames of War

APRIL 23, 1949, marked the first anniversary of the establishment of the PLAN. A flag-presentation ceremony was held on the Yangtze River near Caoxie Gorge in Nanjing. Warships and vessels, 134 in number, formed three formations, and a military band played "Red Navy March." Red carpets covering steel plaques on the warships were removed to reveal exciting names shining bright in the sun: *Jinggangshan Mountain, Gutian, Ruijin, Xingguo, Zunyi, Yenan* and others. The officers and sailors cried out, "Hail! Hail!"

Each warship had been named for a place in China. Frigates were named for large cities like Nan Chang and Guang Zhou. Gunboats were named for smaller cities, like *Yenan* and *Rui Jin*. Landing vessels such as *Jinggangshan Mountain, TaiHang Mountain, Yellow River* and *Huaihe River* commemorated famous mountains and great waters. Naming vessels and warships after mountains and waters in China and places where PLA men have fought heroically means that the officers and sailors can never forget the homeland and will always carry on the glorious traditions of the troops.

The deafening sound of a 21-gun salute was as if thunder were booming and echoing below the clouds. Meanwhile, military music was coming from all directions. Red flags slowly rose high over each warship. The flags of the People's Navy reflected red on the surface of the river.

Under the waving flags, Navy Commander of the East China Military

Zhang Aiping granting commissions

Area Zhang Aiping raised his right fist and took the lead in swearing an oath. It seemed that all the mountains, rivers and seas, the very Earth, were shaking under such sonorous and forceful voices. "Honorary titles are conferred upon us. Our flags flutter in the breeze in splendor and glory. We will prevail in a heroic sea crossing and landing campaign. We will plant the five-starred red flags, signifying the victories of the PLAN in the oceans and rivers around China. We will guard these honorary flags and titles, just as we protect the dignity of our motherland."

Naval Command Born in a Small Village

In March 1949, the mighty PLA army of over one million soldiers arrayed along the north bank of the Yangtze River and prepared to march. All the officers and soldiers were waiting excited and anxious for the order to come from the High Command to "Cross the River." A storm that would sweep across China was forming amidst a seemingly peaceful front line.

The man who would become Defense Secretary of the People's Republic of China (PRC), Zhang Aiping, drove more than 600 miles to the line, from Tianjin to the South, in an American Jeep. The nature and instinct of a military man propelled him to fight alongside his old unit.

The then-39-year-old Zhang Aiping was a renowned general in the East China Field Army. Three years before, he had been injured and sent to the Soviet Union for surgery and rehabilitation. After the operation he convalesced, and, during his three years in the Soviet Union, from time to time he heard news of his former comrades marching forward amid songs of triumph. He dreamed of returning soon to the battlefield.

Finally, while rushing to the Crossing the Yangtze River Campaign burning with impatience, he learned that the dispositions and appoint-

1. AN ARDUOUS BIRTH FROM THE FLAMES OF WAR

ments of the high commanders for this campaign were already in order. It seemed that his chances were slim for leading an army into battle at the front. But he was unwilling to stay in the rear.

After several days of anxiety, Zhang Aiping met with the Commander of the Eastern China Field Army, General Chen Yi. The straightforward general came straight to the point and issued an order. He said, "The Central Military Committee has just decided that the Northeast China Military Area Command will build an air force, while the East China Military Area Command will take charge of building a navy. You will immediately set about establishing the naval force."

The reasons the Central Committee chose the Eastern China Field Army to establish a naval force were as follows: First, east China areas were situated among mountains, rivers and lakes. So if the PLA wanted to liberate these regions, particularly the islands in the southeastern marine areas, it would have to create its own naval force. Second, the KMT naval vessels, military harbors and agencies were located mainly in east China. There was the possibility of inciting defection among these forces and co-opting them into the People's Navy. Third, some PLA troops—such as the Coastal Defense Column in north Jiangsu Province's coastal areas in east China—had had experience in naval battles. It wouldn't take much time for these troops to be transformed into a formal naval force.

Chairman Mao once said humorously, "My cadre policy is to make those with airsickness build an air force and make the ones with seasickness build a navy." There was some helplessness in the humor. Having been stationed a long time at rural bases, the PLA was suddenly being given the mission to build a new arm of service on the eve of a nationwide victory. There must have been a shortage of personnel qualified at an ordinary knowledge level, let alone professionals. Under such circumstance, high commanders who had studied, worked or lived in the Soviet Union naturally formed the first preferred group of talented staff in charge of the newly established naval force, air force and other technical arms. The new naval branch would be constructed following the example of the Red Army in the Soviet Union.

Zhang Aiping had been an elementary school teacher. He could write

Representatives of the PLA board a KMT warship to take it over and inspect it

poems, and his handwriting was very good. Among the high commanders in the PLA at the time, his was a relatively high cultural level and ability to understand. Besides, during his three-year recuperation and stay in the Soviet Union, he had learned a little Russian. So it seemed reasonable that he be responsible for building the Eastern China Navy.

But Zhang Aiping was greatly surprised on hearing of his appointment by General Chen Yi and in a flurry of indecision. All he knew about naval forces was from a book, *Tsushima,* which he'd read several years before. The book was a memoir by a Russian survivor of the Battle of Tsushima during the Japan-Russia War. But such knowledge was way too "amateur" for an ordinary officer or sailor, never mind the commander-to-be of a naval force. So Zhang Aiping was honest with Chen Yi about his limitations, about his ignorance of naval forces, and he suggested that a competent officer be chosen in his place.

But Chen Yi did not accept this. He said, "The Central Committee has already agreed. You need to shoulder this responsibility no matter what."

At the end of the conversation, Zhang Aiping asked a question that he himself considered a bit abrupt. He said, "How does one build a Navy?"

Chen Yi burst into laughter and said, "You'll know it by the time you're done."

On April 23, 1949, the PLA marched across the Yangtze River and conquered the ruling center of the KMT government in Nanjing with a crushing force. This operation marked the defeat and overthrow of the KMT regime. On the same day, over 1,500 officers and troops and 53 warships and vessels from the KMT Navy 2nd Coastal Defense Fleet, along with three fleets led by Fleet Commander Lin Zun and other officers, broke away from the KMT Navy and surrendered to the PLA. The defection and surrender of the KMT naval warships laid the foundation for and facilitated the establishment of the PLAN.

On the same day, at news of the revolt of the KMT 2nd Coastal

Defense Fleet, and receiving instructions from the General Command of the Crossing the Yangtze River Campaign, Zhang Aiping spoke with four PLA officers who came to report.

There were only 13 people at the very beginning of the navy, including Zhang Aiping, those four officers and eight soldiers. As to equipment, all they had were the Jeep driven from Tianjin and two other Jeeps temporarily allocated to them. The 13 personnel and the three Jeeps were the only assets of the Eastern China Navy Command at the beginning. From then on, though, April 23 has been commemorated as the birthday of the People's Navy, and the date will live forever in history.

The general's office was in a small village called Baima Temple, north of the Yangtze River. The founding conference of the Eastern China Navy in this small village more than 60 miles from the sea was brief and clear. That night, Zhang Aiping quickly led his force from Baima Temple to Jiang Yin on the South Bank of the Yangtze. There, in only one week, he reorganized and mobilized the first group of army troops that had been incorporated into the Navy.

While Zhang Aiping and other officers were busy establishing a navy, the KMT troops who had suffered a big defeat on the ground used their

Zhang Aiping lecturing

advantage in the air, searching for and bombing all possible targets from above the Yangtze. They expended all their strength in damaging warships, vessels, docks, ports and shipyards.

Back at Jiang Yin, Zhang Aiping and his comrades heard a piece of unfortunate news. Most of the KMT warships and vessels of the 2nd Coastal Defense Fleet that had defected and had been taken over by the East China Navy had been blown up and damaged by the KMT Air Force. Huge losses had resulted.

At such a moment of frustration, Zhang Aiping couldn't help but remember, "Today I am going to die. What am I thinking now? Certainly many difficulties come at the very beginning, but I will stick to my faith anyhow," part of a poem by his old superior Chen Yi, whom he highly respected. The words had been written during a most difficult and dangerous time. The general had struggled to wage guerrilla war even when surrounded by heavily guarded, hostile troops, and Zhang Aiping had always been moved and inspired by such confidence and lofty sentiment. He felt that the difficulties facing him were insignificant, compared with the dangerous situation Chen Yi had encountered many years before.

Zhang Aiping set out with his command office for Shanghai, where there were various institutions and facilities of the KMT navy. He believed that these were soon to be conquered by the mighty PLA, and he made up his mind to seize warships and recruit personnel there in order to build a PLA naval force as quickly as possible.

"Number 1 Announcement"

Within half a year of marching into Shanghai and stationing there, the Eastern China Navy had taken over more than 30 land-based institutions and facilities, formerly owned by the KMT Navy, spread over five provinces in the East and South of China. Some of the warships and vessels being taken over were damaged or worn out. Altogether, there were 26 warships and 54 boats of various types.

Some of the army commanders were sent to work on the warships

1. AN ARDUOUS BIRTH FROM THE FLAMES OF WAR

and vessels, and they were totally at a loss when confronted with closely packed equipment, meters, thick electric wires and pipelines. They didn't dare touch or move anything. When burrowing down through hatch doors and climbing up stairs, they bumped their heads many times. Out of the activities of such personnel who were lacking in professional knowledge about the navy came frequent reports of warships and vessels striking docks, getting stranded and experiencing operational failures. And the training plans that had been ordered by the Command weren't being finished on time, either.

Zhang Aiping and the Command of the Eastern China Navy knew they had to find workable solutions as quickly as possible.

On June 3, 1949, a sign was placed at 182 Chong Qing South Road in Shanghai that read, "Registry for KMT Navy personnel." And on June 11, 1949, there was an eye-catching recruitment announcement, "Registered Number 1," in the prestigious newspaper, *Ta Kung Pao*, in Shanghai. The announcement stated that "anybody who had served in the KMT Navy could come and register, regardless of rank, no matter whether he had been an officer or sailor, no matter when he had broken away from the KMT, and no matter if he was from navigation, marine

Wearing the new Navy uniform

engine, construction, naval communication, measuring, military supply or medical unit or had worked as other administrative staff."

To seek out able men by publishing ads in *Number 1 Announcement* was an unprecedented recruiting tactic for the CPC-led People's Army. But if they were to build up the People's Navy, the East China Navy had to look everywhere for talent, even by resorting to print ads. The practice was born out of sheer necessity. But it also revealed Zhang Aiping's broad mindedness and boldness of vision.

The PLA Navy is a high-tech armed service. Those new sailors reorganized from the PLA Army without a solid knowledge base or training could barely assume the duty of building a naval force. They had to depend on the officers and troops from the former KMT Navy. Coming even before warships, institutions, factories, docks and other equipment, talent was the most important factor.

After seeing this announcement, soldiers came to the registry to enlist. Now the Command of the Eastern China Navy learned that many of the KMT naval personnel were uncertain about the policies of the PLA and were taking a wait-and-see attitude.

One night, the vice director of the former KMT Navy Office, Xu Shifu, received a visitor who turned out to be Zhang Aiping himself. Xu Shifu was a favorite of former KMT naval commander Gui Yongqing and had once studied in the United States. But one of the PLA's platforms was "Down with U.S. Imperialism!" So Xu Shifu was greatly surprised by Zhang Aiping's visit.

Then, deeply moved by Zhang Aiping's graceful invitation, Xu Shifu finally agreed to join the PLA Navy. Still, Zhang Aiping knew that the other man had another consideration. So he pointed at the light switch and said, "What I require is simple. I don't want my men to know *why* the light is on but only to learn how to *turn* it on." At this, Xu Shifu breathed a sigh of relief and answered repeatedly, "I can help you do this. I can."

The story of Zhang Aiping's paying a nighttime visit to Xu Shifu soon got around and led to strong reaction among the former KMT Naval personnel in Shanghai. Soon more than 1,100 had come to enlist in the PLAN. Some of these new men were experienced naval personnel who had once served in the Beiyang naval forces at the end of the Qing

Dynasty. Eventually, over 4,000 former KMT naval officers and juniors, including the personnel who had defected from the KMT, had joined the PLAN. Among these were dozens who had served as commanding officers, as captains and in higher posts. This represented for the People's Navy an already considerably powerful force, considering the navy had started from nothing.

On August 15, 1949, the East China Navy School was established on the former site of the KMT Navy Command in Nanjing. Zhang Aiping himself served as president. The first 1,500-member group of navy cadets was enrolled. Certain KMT naval officers became instructors. More than 2,000 former KMT naval officers and troops studied mainly the purposes and traditions of the PLA. The school leaders gave lectures. The term was two months.

Zhang Aiping once jokingly explained the goal of the courses offered by the school. He said, "You are lame in one leg, and I am lame in the other. If we two are bound together, we will come up with two healthy legs." The vivid image of "two lame legs" is a reflection of the idea that drawing on others' strong points to make up one's deficiencies, and learning from each other, are the guiding principles of the East China Navy School and in fact of the East China Navy itself.

However, the training plan for new navy men was soon met with a lot of questioning and opposition. The former (defected) KMT Navy general Lin Zun believed that the new men with little educational background were not competent to undertake professional training. Zhang Aiping argued that they could only teach these men to sail a ship first, and improvements could be made later. Lin Zun argued that this was unheard of. The advisors and consultants from the Soviet Union believed, as well, that the Russian navy had never used this approach to train its men.

Zhang Aiping remained unconvinced. He said that all things in the world should be done from scratch.

At that moment, Xu Shifu, who was now the school's education director, stepped in and played an important role. In 1947, he brought a group of former KMT Navy officers and sailors to the United States and took over the repair ship, *Xing'an*. At this point, more than 80 percent of

The East China Navy School, established on the former site of the KMT Navy Command in Nanjing

the men were really newly enlisted. However, after a less than six-month crash course, they were found qualified to do their jobs and to sail the *Xing'an* across the Pacific to China. Xu Shifu then officially presented his painstakingly designed crash-training program, which put an end to the disagreements. The work of training the new cadets was soon on the right path.

Xu Shifu devoted himself wholeheartedly to building the Navy. He tried to find the fastest and most effective ways to teach former Army personnel the skills they needed to sail warships and handle the guns. Later, it was Zhang Aiping who would organize a marriage ceremony for Xu Shifu. In the newly founded China, such an event—a PLAN general's hosting a purely private ceremony for a recruited KMT Navy officer—was remarkable, and for any men, it might have had negative repercussions. In 1998, when Xu Shifu died, Zhang Aiping wrote in sorrow, "Fifty years we have known each other, and I still cherish our friendship the most."

The former KMT Navy officers and sailors were deeply moved by the respect and breadth of thinking of the PLA communists. Their daily life

1. AN ARDUOUS BIRTH FROM THE FLAMES OF WAR

together with these comrades, whom they used to call "Army bumpkins," also exerted a subtle influence on their behavior and ways of thinking.

For example: a former KMT sailor, Zhao Xiao'an, was put into confinement for riotous behavior by the deputy commander of the East China Navy, Lin Zun. An officer named Li Jin was sent by the East China Navy to the defected KMT naval fleet to speak to Zhao Xiao'an. He said to him, "Now you are a member of the Liberation Army. A PLA soldier is not an ordinary soldier. The PLA should overthrow corrupt officials and local tyrants to save all the people suffering in hardship in China. We are both from suffering people, and we were bullied and humiliated by others before this. How can you and the other KMT troops bully other suffering people? To use the words of the PLA, this is a behavior that speaks of forgetting your own suffering and class origins!"

Zhao Xiao'an came from a very poor family. He'd begun to live on the streets when he was a teenager and suffered all kinds of miseries. He enlisted in the KMT Navy to make a living. Inevitably, though, he was affected negatively by old and corrupt soldiers. Such intimate talk as this he had never heard from an officer like Li Jin, and his heart was greatly moved by Li Jin's words. At the moment of grief, the two could

Zhao Xiao'an and others at the Representative Conference of the National Combat Heroes

not help but shed tears. Li Jin then reported to Lin Zun and suggested that since Zhao Xiao'an had already admitted his mistakes and repented, he deserved to be taken out of confinement. But Li Zun said, "Isn't Zhao only a soldier of fortune? How can I break the rules on warships just for him?"

Nevertheless, this so-called soldier of fortune of Lin Zun became in later naval battles one of the first combat heroes of the People's Navy. In 1950, he attended the Representative Conference of the National Combat Heroes and the grand ceremony of National Day, on behalf of the East China Navy. He was even received by the commander-in-chief of the PLA, Zhu De. To this military man who used to be a homeless waif, this was a great encouragement and honor.

On September 23, 1949, when hosting a dinner for 29 defected KMT generals, including Lin Zun, in Beijing (then called Peiping), Chairman Mao said, "Thanks to some of the patriotic men from the KMT Navy, the remnants of the military strength of the KMT rapidly disintegrated and we meanwhile had a rapidly growing air force and naval force."

Trial by Fire

In September 1949, Zhang Aiping—who had represented the Navy at the Chinese People's Political Consultative Conference—was notified by higher-ups that he was being sent to the Soviet Union with a large delegation to negotiate for aid and assistance. He was excited about this and thought there would finally be an opportunity for the East China Navy to improve its warships and equipment.

Among the more than 100 warships and vessels the East China Navy owned at the time, only a dozen could actually be called "warships." Also, many of the ships were only medium in size. The rest were small ships and boats mainly used for defense in the Yangtze River. These worn-out vessels were outdated and performed poorly. The oldest had been in service for more than 50 years. The warships came from many places. Some had been built at the Jiangnan Shipyard during the early period of the Republic of China. Some had been launched during

World War II by the United States, the United Kingdom, France, Japan, Germany, Canada and Australia. There were even old warships that had been bought from Japan at the end of the Qing Dynasty. There were more than 300 kinds of main and auxiliary engines. Many vessels had been neglected for so long that their equipment was badly damaged, and many lacked accessories. For a naval force, such a situation was terrible.

When he returned from the Soviet Union, Zhang Aiping brought just six Soviet naval advisers. It was his conviction that self-help would be better than help from others. He felt that "the best way out is nothing more than self-support." During his more than 30 years as a national defense professional, Zhang Aiping was always a most firm advocate of self-reliance. And so this colored his reaction to the Soviet Union on this visit.

The problem was how to develop and strengthen the Navy, given such a weak foundation, and this was something all East China Navy officers started thinking about.

The former director of the Mechanical Engineering Department of the General Command of the KMT Navy, Rear Admiral Zeng Guosheng, suggested the idea of "out-of-date warships with powerful guns and heavier armor." He thought the priority for the People's Navy should be to eliminate the remnants of the defeated KMT troops along the coast and the Yangtze River, so as to guarantee the security of the waterway and ensure clear and unblocked marine transport. To accomplish this, it would not be necessary to bring large vessels and warships into service. The only concern was how to fight against the large KMT Navy warships in head-on confrontations. It was felt that the only solution would be to rely on more powerful weapons. So it became necessary to refit existing small vessels of low tonnage with cannons and guns of large caliber, wide range and rapid firing rate. In a word, the concept of "out-of-date warships with powerful guns and heavier armor" alluded to equipping small ships with large guns.

Although not all the existing vessels operated properly, they could be refitted. According to Zeng Guosheng, the major difference between merchant ships and warships was the size of the space between compartments. The space on warships is smaller than that on merchant ships.

A minesweeping operation near the mouth of the Yangtze River

This is to prevent warships from being punctured by shots and sinking because of water inflow. Once this principle is grasped, it becomes easy to refit merchant ships to create warships.

The other need was for shipborne guns. Although it was difficult to buy warships, it was still possible to buy shipborne guns. At that time, the War of Liberation had almost ended, and the Army had plenty of ground artillery and large-caliber machine guns that were no longer being used. It wasn't hard to re-equip gun carriages and control aiming systems to mount on boats.

The policy of "out-of-date warships with powerful guns and heavier armor" soon showed its power.

In October 1949, the East China Navy carried out its first combat operation. It sent armed forces to areas of strategic significance near the waters of the Yangtze River and Taihu Lake to eliminate the maritime remnants of the KMT.

At the sight of various kinds of civilian vessels equipped with guns, the enemy became confused, and the Navy was able to attack at close range and take them by surprise. Soon after this, the PLAN assisted the

1. AN ARDUOUS BIRTH FROM THE FLAMES OF WAR

Gunboats pushing forward

Army in advancing to and conquering the islands near the mouth of the Yangtze River and east of Hangzhou Bay, to sweep away the obstacles along the maritime passages near there.

In early 1950, the KMT Navy laid a large amount of naval mines in and outside the mouth of the Yangtze River and threatened to blockade Shanghai, to make this prosperous international metropolitan area a "dead city." During this time, many merchant ships from China and other countries struck the mines. Several foreign merchant ships even sank. Such events caused an uproar in public opinion around the world. Shanghai's mayor, Chen Yi, who was later given the rank of Marshal of the PRC, was anxious about the situation and, together with Zhang Aiping, thrashed out countermeasures. Later he commanded him to remove the naval mines as soon as possible.

In April 1950, the first minesweeping regiment of the Eastern China Navy was established. Six weeks later, this regiment began minesweeping operations at the mouth of the Yangtze River. Actually, the regiment was not a formal one. Ten minesweepers had formerly been 28-ton landing boats. The method to "sweep" mines was rather simple: have two landing boats drag a cable between them to trigger mines along waterways and sea lanes.

During the first half of the first month, the naval forces didn't sweep any mines. The sweeping boats were too small and couldn't carry out the task in the turbulent currents. Besides this, the cables used were so thin that they broke frequently. So the Navy refitted four 420-ton landing ships and equipped them with better minesweeping gear. Thanks to this improvement, these ships were able to sail back and forth and sweep mines day and night. After three months' work, by the end of September the PLAN had finally swept all the underwater mines that had been laid by the KMT Navy.

With this great effort, Shanghai was open to shipping again. The newly born People's Regime had made it through dangerous waters.

The first group of officers and men from the PLA Army who had been trained by the former KMT naval officers fought heroically and skillfully, which astonished their teachers. At that time, the KMT Navy was resorting to frigates of over 1,000 tons and gunboats of hundreds of tons to blockade Mainland China. In sharp contrast, the East China Navy was deploying some landing boats and gunboats of less than 330 tons. So to win the battles, the officers and men of the People's Navy massed many small boats and rushed toward the broadsides of the KMT warships from behind reefs and in darkness. Later, they fired their guns at the KMT warships, and it was like rain pouring down. This was the typical PLA ground military tactic when storming heavily fortified positions. It can be summarized as: Concentrating Fire, Fast Breakthrough, and Going Ahead Full-Blast. Chen Xuejiang, who later became commander of the Fujian Naval Base, was foremost in the fight. He led several small boats and fought fearlessly against the larger warships of the KMT Navy, creating a miracle in the history of the People's Navy, using small boats to defeat large warships.

With the refitting and receipt of warships and vessels of large tonnage, the East China Navy began to target the islands far from the coastline areas occupied by the KMT Navy. First, the naval forces fought in coordination with the Army and attacked the islands in the southeast coastal areas where the KMT Navy was stationed. Later, they marched south and carried out antiblockade battles in coastal areas in Eastern Zhejiang Province. During the first half of 1951, to escort and protect fishing boats, the naval forces in the East China Military Area Command carried out operations to eliminate pirates and KMT remnants between Qing Kou in the north of Jiangsu Province and Sanmen Bay in Zhejiang Province in the south. These operations cut down on KMT harassment to the point where shipping and commercial fishing could resume.

CHAPTER 2

Fierce Battles in Southeast Coastal Areas

ON MAY 7, 1949, just before the PLA troops surrounded Shanghai from all directions and started a general attack, Chiang Kai-shek sailed in melancholy from the city. He made a first stop at the Zhoushan Archipelago and then flew to his final destination, Taiwan.

During 10 years of suppressing bandits and three years of civil war, Chiang Kai-shek and the KMT troops led by him had suffered crushing defeats in the battles against the PLA on Mainland China. The leader would not submit to defeat, though. He hoped instead to use Taiwan as a base and rely on the islands in the southeast coastal areas for counterattack. He made use of the temporary advantages of the KMT Navy and air forces attempting to inflict heavy losses from the sea on the new CPC regime, and he waited for an opportunity.

Encountering the blockades, harassment and invasions by the KMT Navy, the newly founded People's Navy fought back courageously. And after being defeated in the August Sixth Sea Battle and the Naval Battle to the east of Chong Wu, Chiang Kai-shek finally realized that his dream of "counterattacking against the Mainland" was but a castle in the air and that his only choice was to be "content to exercise sovereignty over remote parts and seek self-preservation."

And so a head-on maritime confrontation that had lasted for 15 years was finally ended.

OPENING UP GUANGZHOU'S MARINE GATE

At the end of October 1949, Guangzhou was conquered by the PLA. One of the city's founding fathers, Ye Jianying, was named Mayor of Guangzhou. The city has been the largest commercial port and a sea gate from ancient times. Also, Hong Kong, bordering on Guangzhou, was a transfer station for trade between the newly founded regime and the West. And so the unusual nomination of Ye Jianying as the city's chief executive told of the city's significance to the new regime.

But now this newly liberated city was in a predicament, with its sea gate being blockaded by the KMT. After April 1950, three fleets and one Marine Corps unit of the KMT Navy retreated to the Wanshan Archipelago, not far from the Pearl River Estuary. The Wanshan Archipelago consists of 48 islands 20 to 50 nautical miles from the mainland. Facing Hong Kong and Macao from across the sea, the Archipelago was a choke point for navigation channels and foreign maritime trade for Guangzhou.

To carry out its plan of blockading the mainland, the KMT troops on the Wanshan Archipelago plundered fishermen, extorted "access charges" from the merchant ships that moved frequently between Hong Kong and Macao, and even robbed the ship *Xin Sheng*, out of Hong Kong, of more than 500 liang (about 34.4 pounds) of gold. After that, trade between Guangzhou and areas abroad was cut off. Fishermen dared not go to sea. The city was suffering an increasingly serious economic loss, day after day.

To break through the blockades, open up the southern passage to the sea and remove the barriers outside the Pearl River Estuary were the priorities if there were to be economic recovery and the establishment of international trade for the newly founded PRC. However, it looked as if it would be hard for the newly established River Defense Unit of the Guangzhou Mil-

The marine artery of Guangzhou-Zhujiang

itary Region (later the South China Sea Fleet of the Central South Military area) to accomplish these objectives.

Although the defense unit was able to gather some boats and civilian ships, the total tonnage was barely 1,100 tons. The unit had only three charts and four navigational instruments. Communication between vessels had to rely on infantrymen's walkie-talkies. There was an even larger critical shortage of technical personnel. On average, there was only one mechanical sailor for two vessels and one navigator for three vessels. As to commanding officers or captains experienced in maritime operations, there were only two. Soon after, the command recruited a group of seamen from Wuhan, Changsha and Guangzhou and dispatched 126 Army car drivers to serve as seafaring engineers and helmsmen. By contrast, what the KMT Navy had in its hands was a mighty fleet of more than 30 warships. The tonnage of the KMT Fleet flagship, the frigate *Taihe* alone, outnumbered the total tonnage of the vessels of the PLA River Defense Unit. And even more warships and other vessels from Taiwan were ready to come and lend support at a moment's notice. In a nutshell, the KMT had great advantages not only in tonnage, firepower, numbers and warship speeds but also in the operating skills of its personnel.

And so, unless it adopted an unusual tactic for the first battle, the People's Navy's chances of winning were rather slim.

SMALL BOATS FIGHTING LARGE WARSHIPS

At 2 a.m. on May 25, 1950, under cover of darkness, 16 small boats of the River Defense Unit of the Guangzhou Military Region and eight requisitioned civilian ships prepared to sail to Trash Tail Island, the main anchor station for the KMT Navy. The 24 vessels were grouped into three echelons. The first was the Firepower Echelon: three ships that included the *Guishan* and the *Liberation*. Their mission was to attack the KMT fleet stationed at the anchor grounds of Ma Wan on Trash Tail Island and cover the forces landing on the island. The second was the Covering Echelon, comprised of several vessels, including the gunboats *Struggle* and *Vanguard*. Their duties were to maneuver between Trash Tail

Island and Hong Kong, cover the flanks of the landing troops and intercept escaping KMT troops. The third group, the Landing Echelon, comprised one refitted warship and eight landing boats whose job was to deposit a force of two battalions on Trash Tail Island.

The Firepower Echelon was the first to set sail. According to the original plan, the Landing Echelon and the Covering Echelon would weigh anchor an hour later.

The *Liberation* sailed at the front of the Firepower Echelon. At 4 a.m., the *Liberation* sailed into Ma Wan at Trash Tail Island. Amid the morning mist at sea, Vice Captain Lin Wenhu was startled to discover a dark mass of over 20 to 30 KMT vessels anchored in the naval port.

Martyr Lin Wenhu

Lin Wenhu looked behind him but could see no trace of the other boats.

Before they set out, the Command had ordered each vessel to move at eight knots so that all would land at dawn. But after the *Liberation* set sail, the main engines on some of the other vessels wouldn't start. Some lacked engine oil. Others who were sailing couldn't move at eight knots and were lagging behind. Still others went off-course and ended up at a place over 20 nautical miles from Trash Tail Island. As to the landing forces, due to a lack of knowledge of the tides at the departure point, some of the sailors didn't board in time at high tide and couldn't board at low tide. And so when the *Liberation* was arriving at Ma Wan, the landing boats had not yet sailed, and their personnel were cursing on the shore.

2. FIERCE BATTLES IN SOUTHEAST COASTAL AREAS

This was an emergency for the *Liberation*. There were only one cannon, two machine guns and one temporarily installed recoilless rifle on board. The ship displaced only 31 tons, and its navigational speed was 10 knots. In sharp contrast, the total tonnage of the KMT warships looming out of the mist was over 300 times more.

While Lin Wenhu was still hesitating about what to do, the signalmen on the fleet flagship of the KMT Navy, *Tai He*, sent out a light signal and asked to which part the *Liberation* belonged. It never occurred to them that the newcomer could be a PLA boat.

Lin Wenhu decided immediately to launch a surprise attack with his single warship rather than wait for his comrades to arrive.

The *Liberation* sped to a 325 feet from the left port side of the *Tai He*. Immediately, the guns fired in unison at this frigate with a tonnage of more than 1,500 tons.

The frigate was struck by bullets and bombs. The deck was on fire. The commander of the KMT fleet was severely wounded. In the confusion, the commander of the *Tai He* thought a landing ship near the *Liberation* had surrendered to the People's Navy and started firing at it. But the latter was reluctant to show weakness and responded with fire immediately. Meanwhile, the personnel aboard the other boat believed the *Tai He* had surrendered. They began to kill each other. The shore guns on the island also took part in the confused battle without truly knowing the

The gunboat *Liberation*

situation. Also, the *Liberation* was small and could maneuver easily. It went deep among the KMT boats and engaged in switch-hitting, which made things even more chaotic.

FOREVER HEROES

In the midst of this chaos, some KMT warships fled out of the port of Ma Wan. Meanwhile, the landing ship *Guishan*, of the River Defense Unit of the Guangzhou Military Region, was just arriving and cornered the fleeing KMT with violent firepower. One KMT gunboat was sunk, and many other vessels were struck by bullets and shells. As the sky began to grow lighter, the KMT discovered that they had been up against only one small PLA gunboat and a landing ship of less than 440 tons and still had been fiercely beaten. They immediately retaliated, concentrating fire on those two vessels.

The *Liberation* was struck many times, and 13 of its 19 crewmen were either wounded or killed, including Lin Wenhu himself. The heavily damaged gunboat withdrew from the action but still managed to dodge right and left as it withdrew.

All the KMT vessels then began to fire at the *Guishan*. "The deafening thunder of guns overwhelmed Trash Tail Island. The shells were shot into the water and blew up, causing several tall pillars of water to rise up to the sky. The blood of the wounded stained the deck and the seawater red. In fighting heroically and alone for several hours, the men of the *Guishan* suffered heavy casualties. The ship was severely damaged," notes the diary of one survivor, Cao Zhiyou. Many areas of the ship were on fire. Presently, Guo Qinglong, who was captain of the Firepower Echelon, decided to make an assault landing using the more than 50 army soldiers ready for landing operations in tank cockpits. He sent them to the island despite all the difficulties.

The landing ship *Guishan* successfully struggled to make land among intense enemy firing. Unexpectedly, though, a large fire sealed the hatch closed, and nothing could be done to open it, no matter how hard the crew and the soldiers tried. Clouds of smoke were filling the burning

2. FIERCE BATTLES IN SOUTHEAST COASTAL AREAS

The landing ship *Guishan* being sunk

cabin. The temperature was rising fast. The threat of death overhung the soldiers inside.

At this critical moment, a heroic engineer, Wen Guoxing, threw himself at the hatch and turned the handle with all his strength. The hatch finally opened, but Wen Xingguo was burned cinder-black, and his body was fused to the hatch.

Freed at last, the soldiers charged the beachhead. Intense KMT firing began from various light and heavy weapons. The record tells us that, after the battle, only five seriously wounded men survived among the 78 soldiers from the *Guishan*.

While the *Guishan* was drawing all the KMT fire and fighting its bloody battle, the PLAN Cover and Landing echelons seized the opportunity to land soldiers on the Green Islet (Qing Zhou Dao) and on Triangle Island (San Jiao Dao). These men pressed onward to the islands of the Wanshan Archipelago under cover provided by the artillery and navy and defeated the counterattack of the KMT 3rd Fleet. After more than two months' fighting, all the islands and islets in the archipelago had been liberated by the People's Navy. The passageway to the sea in Guangzhou had been opened up, the blockade removed.

A decommissioned *Liberation* is on display today in the square of the Chinese Navy Museum in Qingdao. Trash Tail Island has been renamed Laurel Mountain Island (Guishan Island), to commemorate the heroic deeds of the *Guishan*. A huge rock on the beachhead battlefield is engraved, "The landing site of the heroes of the ship *Guishan*." Another monument nearby is engraved, "Eternal Life for the martyrs who liberated Trash Tail Island."

Breaking through the Blockade: Naval Campaign near East Zhejiang Province

Zhejiang Province, along the East China Sea, is one of the smallest provinces of Mainland China, but it includes the most islands and reefs in the nation.

In the 1950s, the KMT Navy occupied some islands in the coastal areas of East Zhejiang Province as a strong point, and they unceasingly harassed and sabotaged mainland coastal areas. They also pirated foreign merchant ships and attempted to create disturbances and provoke international conflicts. In 1952, the KMT Navy took over a British merchant ship and killed its captain, Robert Adams. In October 1953, they seized the Polish tanker *Praca*, and in 1954 they took the Polish merchant ship *President Gottwald* and the Soviet tanker *Tuapse*. Premier Zhou Enlai's heart was torn with anxiety. He sent several telegrams to the East China Military Area to inquire about the situation and tried to come up with a countermeasure.

At that time, the waters between the Dachen Islands and the Yushan Islands, in the coastal area of Zhejiang, were controlled by the KMT Navy. If the People's Navy was to break through the blockades and resist the coastal area harassment, there was only one way to go, and that was to conquer the islands.

Although the KMT forces retreated to Taiwan, they still put up stubborn resistance at strategic positions at sea. And being stationed on coastal islands near Zhejiang, Fujian and Guangdong provinces, they were ready to harass and sabotage the People's Navy at any time. They even attempted to launch a counterattack on Mainland China.

2. FIERCE BATTLES IN SOUTHEAST COASTAL AREAS

A warship fleet in combat

SINKING THE KMT NAVY ESCORT TAIPING

The Dachen Islands area is the largest fishing ground in Zhejiang Province. It abounds with many species of fish. Every year during flood season a large number of fishing boats gather in the area. At the peak, there are as many as 5,000 boats carrying more than 100,000 fishermen.

In the early morning of March 18, 1954, fishing boats sailing out from Mainland China were harassed and damaged by two KMT warships. The East China Navy then sent out two warships to protect the fishing and to fight the KMT warships. Meanwhile, nearby People's Navy patrol boats were attacked and harassed by six KMT aircraft.

The East China Military Command immediately gave combat orders to the People's Navy. People's Naval Aviation sent two MiG-15 (Mikoyan-Gurevich) fighters into the sky above Nantian where they encountered four KMT F-47s. The dogfights between the two PLAN MiG-15 fighters and the four KMT F-47 fighters continued into the skies over the Dachen Archipelago. The MiGs pressed on toward the F-47s and fired at them when 230 feet above the sea and with only a quarter-mile between them. During the entire air battle, more than 10,000 fishermen working in nearby waters looked up to the sky and watched. When the PLAN won, great cheers burst from the onlookers. This had been an unprecedented spectacle in the history of world naval and air battles.

A battle group of torpedo boats breaking the waves

The Nantian Air Battle was the first in which PLA Naval Aviation had participated since its founding. Two KMT aircraft were shot down. People's Naval Aviation suffered no casualties. The score was now 2—0, with the PLA ahead. After this, the KMT and the PLA began fighting for control of sea and sky in the waters of East Zhejiang Province. The Battle of Dachen Archipelago unfolded.

In April 1954, the PLAN's 31st Patrol Torpedo Boat Squadrons, stationed at Qingdao, received a sudden order to relocate. After several days of transport, the squadrons finally learned that their destination was Zhejiang Province.

This was a top-secret operation.

At the time, the largest warship on either side in east China's Zhejiang Province area was the KMT Navy escort *Taiping*, a ship that often flaunted its huge size and went rushing and swerving madly about. With a full-load, this leviathan displaced 1,430 tons. It was equipped with 18 cannons of calibers ranging from 76.2mm, to 40mm to 20 mm. More

2. FIERCE BATTLES IN SOUTHEAST COASTAL AREAS 29

than 220 crewmen served on the *Taiping*. At the time, it was one of the KMT's frigates with the strongest firepower. (Other KMT warships were also of large tonnages and strong firepower.) The ordinary vessels of the East China Navy simply could not harm them. This was the reason a fleet of PT-boats from the PLAN's 31st Patrol Torpedo Boat Squadrons was dispatched there, to await the opportune moment to attack the large- and medium-scale warships of the KMT Navy.

The PLAN torpedo boats were Type 123 Soviet speedboats. Their standard displacement was only 22.86 tons, and their navigational speed was 52 knots. There were two torpedo tubes and two 12.7-mm dual-barreled antiaircraft machine guns. Because of its small body, this kind of torpedo boat was a high-speed, flexible . . . and highly lethal vessel. For these reasons, they were called the Iron Fist.

One day in mid-May 1954, the PLAN launched a combat operation to take the Dongji Islands. At early dawn the day after, the KMT dispatched four warships, including the flagship *Taihe*. The two sides engaged in distant fighting due to bad weather and low visibility. The Naval Battle around the Dongji Islands attracted the attention of Zhang Aiping, commander-in-chief on the front lines in Zhejiang Province. After checking his information, he determined to bombard and sink one or two KMT medium- or large-sized warships.

The PLAN's 31st Patrol Torpedo Boat Squadrons were lurking near the Dongji Islands, ready to round up KMT warships under the guidance of radar stations on nearby High Island. But no trace of the KMT fleet could be found. The PLA would wait nearly half a year for a face-to-face encounter with its KMT rivals.

One day at the end of October, the PLAN PT-boats received intelligence about the location of the KMT warships. Under cover of darkness, six PT-boats from the 31st Patrol Torpedo Boat Squadrons, towed by the Escort Boat Squadron, set sail to new standby positions. On the route they chose there was little sign

Torpedo boat formation

of other boats coming and going, so there was little possibility of their being discovered. Besides, during the nighttime navigation, when the visual range was poor, the small torpedo boats could hide behind the large escort boats, which made them even more "invisible." In this way, six PT-boats were able to sail to High Island's anchoring grounds without being noticed and could hide opposite the islands occupied by the KMT Navy.

On November 3, a large KMT Navy warship appeared in the predetermined attack area. Six PT-boats immediately set sail as straight as arrows toward the ship. At that time, though, the winds and waves at sea were above sea state 4 (on the World Meteorological Organization Sea State scale). In such conditions, the accuracy of torpedoes can't be guaranteed. And so six PT-boats had no choice but to take cover and await another chance to attack.

By now it was already early winter. There were no accommodations or sleeping bunks on the narrow torpedo boats. The men stood at post, then curled up with their clothes on. They installed a board on deck to be used as a sleeping bunk, due to the lack of space. When it rained, the men had to wear rain jackets and stand in the weather because there was no place to take shelter. Soon they were soaked. Every time a cutting wind blew, they trembled with cold. A shivering frost covered their bodies, and their faces were blue. A sailor said, "Except for a fervent heart, I felt as it I were soaking in ice water." It was also impossible to cook on the boats, so eating became a major issue. There was no alternative but to send men a good distance in landing boats, to cook. When the meals were ready, they were brought to the torpedo boats, but because of the cold wind and far distances, when the dishes finally arrived they were ice-cold.

Despite all these terrible hardships, though, the sailors on the torpedo boats believed that a common will was as strong as a city bulwarks. They were determined to wait until they saw their chance.

Shortly after midnight on November 14, the High Island radar discovered a KMT warship coming from the Dachen Islands. The radar technicians were staring at a tiny point of light on the screen. The recorders reported instantly in what direction the warship was moving

2. FIERCE BATTLES IN SOUTHEAST COASTAL AREAS

and how far away it was. The draftsmen then located the ship on a sea chart. Later, the head of communications informed the torpedo boats of the route of the KMT warship.

At the command, four PLAN torpedo boats sailed out of the bay at full speed and straight at the target. But the torpedo boats could not knife through the water. Now they were lifted to the crests of waves, now plunged into the troughs. The spoondrifts they created splashed over the decks. These boats were less than 65 feet long, and there was a distance of just 65 to 100 feet between swells. When a boat was at the end of the last swell, it was dropped into a trough and the rest of the boats pressed the bow. The deck was submerged. At such a moment, a torpedo boat couldn't plow through the waves but only move forward by semi-submerging and wave breaking. To sail in such conditions, the loads of the main engines increased and clunking rumbles could be heard.

Meanwhile, the boatswains and torpedo men, standing at the most dangerous positions, were lashed tightly to the rail of the navigation bridge to prevent them from being swept into the sea.

Soon, though, the officers and crew were no longer conscious of the danger. Their only thought was to get near the KMT warship.

When they were six or seven nautical miles away, the men on the torpedo boats could see clearly the bridge, the anchor and the radar on the warship. At that moment, though, the warship had no idea that misfortune would soon befall it. It saw itself sailing east without fuss or incident. But when only four nautical miles separated the four PTs from the KMT warship, the torpedo boats immediately formed a battle formation. At the command of the captain on each boat, the bodies of the torpedo boats shook fiercely in unison as eight torpedoes went whistling out toward the KMT warship.

Illuminated projectiles and signal flares were launched from the warship and streaked into the night sky. At daybreak, on the side of the KMT warship, now about to capsize, the characters spelling out *Taiping* were still clearly visible. This leviathan, that had until now rampaged around the waters of the Dachen Archipelago, finally sank into the sea after hours of struggle to stay afloat. Twenty-nine KMT naval officers and men died, 37 were wounded, and 145 were rescued.

The *Taiping* sinking

This was the first time the People's Navy torpedo boats went into battle. Thanks to enough preparation and appropriate positions for hiding, the boats took their rival by surprise in close combat and night action and saw great success. The *Taiping* was the largest vessel to have been sunk by the PLAN to that time.

A WONDER BY A SINGLE PT-BOAT

In late November 1954, six speedboats from the 1st Patrol Torpedo Boat Fleet of the East China Navy sailed to standby locations near Baiyan Shan Island under the cover of several escort boats. The places they were headed were the best for surrounding the strategic passage around the upper and lower Dachen Islands. The PLAN's 31st PT-Boat Squadrons had sunk the destroyer escort *Taiping* not long before, and the officers and sailors of the 1st Fleet were motivated by such heroic deeds and not willing to lag behind. They were determined to show their own abilities.

After they struggled to take cover for more than 40 days, chance favored the PLAN at last.

2. FIERCE BATTLES IN SOUTHEAST COASTAL AREAS 33

On January 10, 1955, massive waves roiled the waters of east China's Zhejiang Province. The wind speed was 56 feet/sec. The KMT warships anchored in the Dachen Islands to get out of the wind. At noon, People's Naval Aviation dispatched several fighter planes for a massive bombing raid on the warships, a joint operation with the People's Air Force. Many KMT warships and other vessels were sunk or damaged. The harbor was in flames. The surviving ships fled in disorder and retreated against the weather to the southwest, to the open sea.

The men of the 1st PT-boat Fleet, lying in ambush at the anchor grounds at Baiyan Shan Island, had been waiting for just this moment. They knew that after sunset those escaping warships would try to return to base port, and that the passageway outside Baiyan Shan Island was the only way they could pass. It was the best position for a torpedo boat to ambush a warship.

At dusk, Fleet command sent out a warning: the KMT warships that had been escaping to the open sea to avoid bombardment from the air were about to come back. The PLAN ships were ordered to prepare to attack. Ten minutes later, four torpedo boats from the 1st Fleet sailed from Baiyan Shan Island to their rally points. Due to harsh conditions at sea, two of the boats fell behind.

On receiving the order to attack, PT-boat #102 dashed at the KMT warships at 30 knots. When the boat was 30 cable lengths away (one cable is 608 feet), Vice Captain Wang Zhengxiang gave the order to prepare to fire two torpedoes, as per regulations. The boat then drew near a KMT warship and sailed with it in the same direction for two minutes. When Captain Zhang Yimin attempted to fire, however, he discovered that the torpedo from one tube was shot out unusually slowly and the one from the other tube couldn't be launched at all.

Almost at the same time, PT-boat 101 also launched torpedoes at the KMT warships. But due to strong winds and big waves, two torpedoes strayed off-target.

Zhang Yimin was anxious now and immediately shut down his engine. He ordered that the obstacles inside the torpedo tubes be cleaned out. Two torpedo men lay down on the frozen deck and struggled to do this. Finally, they found the cause of the malfunctions. With such big

Zhang Yimin commanding in battle

waves pounding the boat, as soon as the front tube covers were removed, a lot of water poured in. The gunpowder needed to propel the torpedoes became damp and couldn't burn completely. As a result, there wasn't enough gas pressure, and the torpedoes couldn't be launched properly.

After troubleshooting the right torpedo tube, Zhang Yimin ordered his sailors to start the main engine. They then chased their target toward the Dachen Islands. But after about 15 minutes of this they were ordered to return to the original anchoring point. Everybody on board was vexed at being forced to let the KMT warship flee, since they had seen the ship as something already in their back pocket.

About two hours later, radar again captured a trace of a KMT warship. The Captain of the 1st PT-boat Fleet shouted out an order: "Numbers 105 and 106, attack!"

On hearing this order, Zhang Yimin rushed to the Command to ask permission for PT-boat 102 to attack again as well.

At this moment, though, there were torpedoes only in the right tube on boat 102. It is self-evident that a one-ton torpedo will exert great influence on the balance of a torpedo boat of only 22 tons. Worse, due to the strong winds, large waves and low visibility, there was a high risk of crewmen dying and ships capsizing. And so the captain of the 1st PT-boat fleet did the reasonable thing and refused Zhang Yimin's request.

But Zhang Yimin, spirit soaring, would not be put off and continued to request permission to attack. Finally, he was told to go ahead.

At 11:02 p.m., PT-boat 102 once again set sail. This was seven or eight minutes after PT-boats 105 and 106 had sailed. There were 5–6 Bft north winds and rapid wave action. Amid the raging torrents, boat 102 started to heel over fiercely. Five crewmen leaned to port to keep the boat from

2. FIERCE BATTLES IN SOUTHEAST COASTAL AREAS

capsizing. Worse, in the midst of this peril, boat 102 wasn't finding any trace of PT-boats 105 and 106 at the attack point, and Zhang Yimin was thinking, "Maybe I'll have to attack all alone, this time."

The moon emerged and shone on the surface if the water. PT-boat 102 was sailing toward it. After moving along at high speed for about 15 minutes, the target loomed. It was the KMT gunboat *Lingjiang*. Formerly named *Dongting*, this was an American gunboat using an internal combustion engine and having a full-load displacement of only 500 tons. It drew just 6.6 feet of water. Strictly speaking, torpedoes were meant for attacking a surface warship more than 325 feet long and with a tonnage of over a 1,100 tons. But here at sea, at this moment, no such stipulations occurred to Zhang Yimin. His only thought was to "Attack and attack!"

Because of the noise suppressor on Number 102, sailing at 35 knots the boat was able to get close to the *Lingjiang* without being noticed. When only five chains separated the two vessels, Zhang Yimin told himself to keep calm. "There was only one torpedo. We had to fire accurately from a short distance."

When there was but three chains between the two vessels, Zhang Yimin aimed the torpedo sight. At this point, the boatswain Zhang Deyu was shouting persistently, "Captain, it's time to fire!"

Zhang Yimin, however, was taking his time. He waited until his boat was less than 1,000 feet from the KMT warship. The angle between the two was about 60 degrees. He ordered while aiming, "Get ready! Fire!"

As the torpedo moved through the water, PT-boat 102 reduced speed at once, shut down the engine to move in reverse, and then turned hard to port and withdrew. Within 10 seconds, all the glasses and security lampshades on board were shattered by the explosion when the torpedo reached its target. According to an expert, PT-boat 102 would have perished that day along with the KMT warship if it had been just 100 feet closer to the detonation point.

This torpedo boat, Number 102, which would be involved in many maritime battles, was given the honorific "Heroic Torpedo Speed Boat" after this incredible encounter. PT- boat 102 was a living symbol of the spirit of the PLAN.

TARGET, YIJIANGSHAN ISLANDS!

After the sinking of the destroyer escort *Taiping* and the gunboat *Lingjiang* by the PLAN torpedo boats, the remaining warships deployed by the KMT Navy around the waters near the Dachen Archipelago trembled with fear at even the mention of the PLAN. There was no way they would take reckless action now. Naval supremacy was now in the hands of the PLAN.

Likewise, after many battles, supremacy in the air was also in the hands of the People's Air Force and Naval Aviation.

With naval and air supremacy in hand, the next objective of the PLAN was to conquer the Dachen Archipelago.

The Yijiangshan Islands, the barrier to the north of the Archipelago, became the primary target during the Battle of Dachen Archipelago. Once having taken and passed through the Yijiangshan Islands, the PLAN would be overlooking the Archipelago and could take it easily.

The Yijiangshan Islands are two islets divided by a long, narrow trench. The islands are bounded by steep cliffs such that the appearance is that of a huge rock standing erect over the sea. The seawater flowing between the two islets like a river divides them into South River Area

PLA Naval Aviation launching an attack

2. FIERCE BATTLES IN SOUTHEAST COASTAL AREAS 37

and North River Area. The name of the islands translates One River and Hills Islands and is derived from this unique topography.

At the time of the battle, these islands, occupying only half a square mile, were thickly dotted with 154 blockhouses and underground bunkers. Atop the surrounding rocks, tier upon tier of firing ports had been carved out. All the nearby shoals where vessels could dock were laid over by underwater mines and obstacles.

This area would be the first battlefield for a joint operation by the Army, the Navy and the Air Force. The then defense secretary, Peng Dehuai, ordered the command post at the front to use a sledgehammer to kill a fly.

While the battle plan was being drawn up, there was a bitter dispute. The Soviet military advisor strongly argued that the PLAN should sail at night and land at daybreak. He cited the Allied landing at Normandy, the landing on Sicily and the Battle of Okinawa during World War II to make his point that nighttime sailing and daybreak landing was the only way to win a battle for the Yijiangshan Islands, because PLAN warships under sail could then escape harassment by KMT planes and warships. Some Army commanders participating in battles to liberate islands along the southeastern coast of Mainland China agreed with him because they were good at night fighting.

But the commander of the East China Navy, Tao Yong, was against this plan. He thought it would be even harder to sail at night than in daylight because of the performance differences among the warships of the East China Navy as well as their lack of experience in coordinated operations. With air and naval supremacy already in hand, he felt the PLAN could land in the daytime. He said it would be especially advantageous to set sail at noon and land in the afternoon, when the tide was in.

There was now a standoff. The Soviet military advisor stormed out the door in the heat of the moment. Tao Yong would not yield.

It had been decided by Chairman Mao Zedong that Tao Yong would serve in the Navy. During the time of the New Fourth Army, he had led a sea defense unit in a fight with the Japanese Navy in onshore and offshore areas. In 1949, during the Crossing-the Yangtze River Campaign, when the British frigate HMS *Amethyst* was bombing the PLAN, he had deployed gunners to fight back, forcing the frigate to wave the white flag. After this, Chairman Mao joked, "Tao Yong is a daring man with great skills. Let him distinguish himself in the Navy." And so in 1952, soon after coming home from the Korean battlefield, he was made commander of the East China Navy.

Daytime navigation required a lot of support by various kinds of landing craft. According to the combat plan, for the Yijiangshan Sea-Crossing and Landing Battle at least 125 kinds of warships and other vessels would be needed. But there were only 59 vessels in the East China Navy. Although it had requisitioned 60 more, they were still short. So 17 landing boats were borrowed from the Shanghai Jiangnan Shipyard and Shanghai Port Authority. Leading up to the Battle of the Yijiangshan Islands, the East China Navy called up 144 warships and vessels of various types.

Firepower is the most important issue during a landing operation—landing forces are like sitting ducks, totally exposed at sea. So it is imperative to neutralize the enemy with strong firepower. After landing and marching inland deep and wide, when coast artillery and naval forces far away on the shore can't neutralize the enemy with firepower coverage, the accompanying guns from the warships should fire randomly at targets. For this reason, it is vital to strengthen the firepower on warships. So Katyusha rocket launchers were moved from the armory to the warships, and the landing and shipping boats were refitted to make them firepower ships. Tao Yong and his deputy, Peng Deqing, were in command in Shanghai. In 21 days, 77 vessels were refitted.

During the course of a freezing winter in the waters near the Dachen Islands, there were strong winds and big waves. All fishing boats suspended operations. The KMT naval forces thought they could relax for a while, as it would be impossible for the PLAN to carry out landing operations during this season. Who would dare to cross the sea against a wild wind howling day and night and through code-6 and -7 swells? According to analysis by the U.S. advisory group, with the available worn-out vessels and navigation instruments it would be impossible for PLA naval and air forces to carry out a sea crossing and landing operation during such windy and rainy winter.

2. FIERCE BATTLES IN SOUTHEAST COASTAL AREAS

The Army and Navy on the way to the Yijiangshan Islands in a coordinated operation

But the Americans were wrong.

At 9:00 a.m. on January 18, 1955, there sounded a roar from a distant airborne plane. In an instant, the Yijiangshan Islands were shrouded in smoke and glowed with fire. After 9:00 a.m., all was suddenly hushed. Smoke and dust were blown away by the wind, and the Islands became faintly visible again amidst a lingering haze.

There was then a deadly silence on the parts of both the KMT and the PLA. Even the sea seemed strangely quiet as waves rolled in peacefully in dazzling sunlight.

At 12:05 p.m., there came the sudden violent roar of guns. Bombs and shells rained down on the Yijiangshan Islands. The sky and the sea trembled, and the Yijiangshan Islands became burning islands.

Ten minutes after the first round of artillery fire, under the cover and support of over 180 PLAAF and Naval Aviation combat aircraft, 46 of the PLAN's 142 combat vessels carrying the Army crossed the sea. In mighty formation, the landing vessels pressed onward to the Yijiangshan Islands, now shrouded once more by smoke. They would land at high tide.

The main landing point was a protected area northwest of the Yijiangshan Islands, an area that wouldn't work for the usual landing procedures. There were jagged rocks of grotesque shape, like the teeth of sharks, coming up out of the water. Waves and whirlpools bounced off the rocks. People sweated over passing through this area even at ordinary times.

It was at just such a strategically "impossible" place, where the KMT defending troops would naturally drop their guard and cut back on fire control, that several PLAN landing boats sailed straight in, close against the rocks and the cliffs, to ensure that their men could land on the islands. According to KMT officer memoirs, the PLAN forces simply popped up atop the top the rocks across the sea. It was a terrible moment for the KMT. They could not have known that for several months the People's Navy and Army had repeatedly drilled on this very action. Just over three hours later, the Yijiangshan Islands had been basically conquered by the PLAN. More than 1,000 KMT defending troops had been killed.

After the liberation of the Yijiangshan Islands, the KMT saw its presence in the Dachen Islands as imperiled. Soon, the defending KMT troops abandoned the Dachen Islands and withdrew to Taiwan. By this time, all the islands occupied by the former KMT Navy in coastal areas east of Zhejiang Province were in the hands of the PLA.

The August Sixth Sea Battle

Starting in early 1960, the government of the Republic of China (Taiwan authority) frequently dispatched warships and delivered small groups of armed spies to look for opportunities to harass the coastal areas of Mainland China. In 1965, the two sides fought three sea battles in succession. Among these, the August Sixth Sea Battle was the biggest, and it was also the biggest PLAN victory.

Further, the three naval defeats came as severe blows to the KMT Navy in Taiwan, altering the military balance across the Taiwan Strait.

2. FIERCE BATTLES IN SOUTHEAST COASTAL AREAS

With the defeats, the dominance of the KMT Navy over the Taiwan Strait was a thing of the past.

LOCKING IN THE TARGET

At 6:00 p.m. on August 5, 1965, the commander of the South Sea Fleet (SSF) of the People's Navy, Wu Ruilin, had just come home from the office when he received an urgent phone call from Fleet operations, apprising him of an updated enemy status. He rushed to operations, where the chief on duty reported that two ground radar stations had discovered two KMT warships 84 nautical miles from the port of Zuoying, in Taiwan, blending into a group of fishing ships as they approached the Mainland.

Wu Ruilin immediately ordered the first echelon, four high-speed escort boats and six torpedo ships, to take cover in Qing'ao Bay at Nan'ao Island, and the second echelon, gunboat 161 and another five torpedo boats to stand by as reinforcements.

According to intelligence received later, the two KMT warships coming to attack were the patrol ship *Jianmen*, with a standard displacement of 595 tons, and the sub-chaser *Zhangjiang*, displacing 298 tons. After setting sail, the two boats had shut down their on-board communications systems for fear of being detected by PLA radar. They also detoured to the open seas at Hong Kong and from there moved on to Dongshan Island. But they were discovered by the PLAN, anyway, despite all the intrigues and wiles.

With the approach of darkness, several mysterious figures on the *Zhangjiang* put on PLA

The KMT warship *Zhangjiang*

uniforms. These were KMT special troops who would attempt to land near Dongshan Island in Fujian Province to sabotage the radar stations there.

At 12:31 a.m. on August 6, the PLAN escort and the torpedo boats were scheduled to gather. However, although they weren't far apart, due to a navigational error the two battle groups did not meet.

At 1:40 a.m., the two targeted KMT warships discovered the approaching PLAN escort boat formation and fired illuminating projectiles at them. The commander of the echelon, Kong Zhaonian, ordered his group to make close contact with the KMT warships at high speed but not open fire. So each escort boat sailed at high speed toward the two KMT vessels while evading KMT bombs, so as to separate the *Zhangjiang* and the *Jianmen*.

The original PLAN idea had been to attack the *Jianmen* first, but the ship fired back and then fled east at high speed. So Kong Zhaonian decided to go after the *Zhangjiang*, which was closer.

The escort boats moved to about three chains from the *Zhangjiang* and began going in the same direction and shooting at it violently. (The closest distance between the two at any point would barely exceed one cable length, or 608 feet.) The firepower of the *Zhangjiang* was neutralized. The guns fitted on the PLAN escort boats were of small caliber, but their firing rate was very high. Added to this, due to the simultaneous discharge of guns on these boats from a combat formation, shells poured onto the *Zhangjiang* like countless hailstones. Still, it wasn't easy for small escort boats to sink the much larger *Zhangjiang*, which was like a big honeycomb with dozens of enclosed inner cabins, which made it even more difficult to sink.

Still, where were the torpedo boats? Well, it seems that, in the "dark" due to backward telecommunication equipment

The KMT warship *Jianmen*

2. FIERCE BATTLES IN SOUTHEAST COASTAL AREAS

and their lack of experience in coordinated sea operations, the torpedo boats were lagging behind, and so they were late in showing up.

Finally, though, two torpedo boats of the 3rd Attack Team caught up and attacked. But their efforts were in vain. In the darkness, they mistook a nearby island reef for their target, due to target identification errors. Soon after this, two torpedo boats from the 1st Attack Team came to assist, but the four torpedoes they launched were all evaded by the *Zhangjiang*.

After an hour's fierce fighting, the *Zhangjiang* had still not been sunk.

When the intelligence on this reached the combat room of the PLA escort fleet, the atmosphere grew tense. Wu Ruilin ordered the escort boats to chase the *Zhangjiang* and fire armor-piercing shells below its waterline. Then the PLAN made four more attacks on the ship. They began to fire from 550 yards and continued until they were within just over 330 yards away. Ten minutes after this, the *Zhangjiang* exploded and sank at last from the repeated attacks.

PURSUING AND ATTACKING THE *JIANMEN*

It was early morning on August 6, 1965. Dawn was breaking over the sea. After the *Zhangjiang* sank, the *Jianmen* lingered in the area, though it dared not try to rescue the officers and men on the *Zhangjiang* nor try to flee to Taiwan. Meanwhile, the KMT Air Force could get quickly into the air over the waters here near Taiwan, so if the PLA escort boats couldn't sink the *Jianmen* fast, all would be exposed to KMT attacks from the air. The atmosphere in the Fleet combat room was intense, with everybody asking whether to fight.

This critical situation led to a ripple effect at the Headquarters of the General Staff in Beijing. Deputy Chief of General Staff Li Tianyou called Wu Ruilin and asked him whether they should fight.

Wu Ruilin's reply was a brief but resolute "Keep fighting."

After receiving such an order, echelon commander Kong Zhaonian first commanded escort boat 611 to return to port to repair severe damage: during the battle in which the *Zhangjiang* had sunk, the escort

High-speed gunboat firing and covering torpedo boats launching torpedoes

boat had been struck by 17 shells and almost half the crew had been lost. Three main engines out of four had been damaged. The engineer, Mai Xiande, had suffered a severe head wound, though after being bandaged he was able to stand fast at his post, determined to operate the engines in the forward and aft engine rooms. He even sailed the boat on its return to port. He was later awarded the honorary title "Combat Hero" by the Ministry of National Defense.

Kong Zhaonian then ordered three high-speed escort boats and five torpedo boats from the second echelon of speedboats to form a new attack formation to pursue the *Jianmen*. When there was 50 chains' distance between the two vessels, the *Jianmen*'s artillery began to fire at the pursuing high-speed escort boats. Countless shells fell into the water near the echelon. When they were at 20 chains apart, the speedboat echelon still didn't return fire. When the distance was seven chains, the three escort boats continued to move in the same direction as the *Jianmen* and at the same speed. It was at this moment that Kong Zhaonian ordered his men to fire. The three boats began to concentrate violent fire on the *Jianmen*. After only five minutes, the ship was set ablaze. Four minutes later, a big fire could be seen on the deck. With flames roaring, the ship couldn't fight back.

Meanwhile, the torpedo boat formation of the second echelon had come to provide support. Kong Zhaonian ordered the escort boat formation to leave the best attack positions and the torpedo boat formation to launch torpedoes right away. When there were only two chains between these boats and the *Jianmen*, the formation launched 10 torpedoes, three of which were direct hits. The *Jianmen* sank rapidly, and the explosion caused huge radiating waves. PT-boat No.109, closest to the Jianmen, shook violently, the telecommunications man was thrown from his seat and the transmitter key was jettisoned into the sky.

After the *Jianmen* had been sunk, Kong Zhaonian received an order to return to port immediately. The KMT Navy in Taiwan had just sent four aircraft to join the battle. But Kong Zhaonian could see that many

KMT men had been thrown into the water by the explosion. Out of a double concern—humanitarianism and acquiring intelligence from captives—he asked the escort boats to pick up the surviving KMT men.

When the four KMT aircraft appeared in the sky above the battle area, which was now a salvage spot, eight PLAAF fighters appeared in the sky as well and the KMT was forced to run.

During the August Sixth Sea Battle, the SSF of the PLAN sank the KMT Navy's warships *Jianmen* and *Zhangjiang*. The KMT commander, Rear Admiral Hu Jiaheng, and over 170 officers and men were killed. The captain of the *Jianmen*, Wang Yunshan, and over 33 officers and men were captured. By contrast, four PLAN crewmen died that day, only 28 were injured, and just two escort boats and two torpedo boats were damaged.

CHAPTER 3

Safeguarding Sovereignty over the South China Sea

ON MAY 3, 1975, at the end of a meeting with the Political Committee of the Navy, Chairman Mao Zedong said, "Our Navy is only this big," gesturing with the little finger of his left hand. Twenty-two years before, he had inspected the Navy for the first time and written, "In order to oppose Imperialist aggression, we must construct a powerful naval force."

In his youth, Mao had seen the military prowess of foreign warships in the inland branches of the Xiangjiang River. Such inveterate hatred was one of the reasons he and his comrades had devoted themselves to revolution. The newly founded People's Republic must build a mighty naval force to guard its vast coastal areas and territorial seas, so as not to repeat the disastrous blunders of modern China.

However, given the weak industrial base and low overall national strength at the time, the People's Navy was able to build a maritime combat force capable only of offshore defense using lightweight warships and other vessels. During its battles with foreign invaders, though, such a small force was able not only to fulfill its sacred mission to protect the motherland but also to leave many records in the history books of world naval and maritime warfare.

Every Chinese army man is tremendously proud of these heroic deeds.

Air Battles above Hainan Island

In August 1964, the Gulf of Tonkin Incident (also known as the Beibu Gulf Event)—later revealed to have been fabricated—was reported and shocked the world, leading to an escalation in the action of the Vietnam War.

While the U.S. began the wanton and indiscriminate bombing of northern Vietnam, they also did continuous reconnaissance on and harassment of Hainan Island, adopting the so-called sideswipe tactic. In other words, they flew along the boundary of Chinese territorial waters and crossed the line from time to time. Then they flew out over the high seas whenever Chinese aircraft showed up and waited for opportunities to come back when the Chinese left.

Unable to tolerate combat aircraft from other countries flying wantonly over its territorial waters, the Chinese government planned a counterattack.

CHALLENGING THE CEILING HEIGHT

In November 1964, a piece of intelligence about U.S. aircraft carrying out air reconnaissance in Chinese airspace above Hainan Island arrived on Mao Zedong's desk from the Headquarters of the General Staff. After reading it, Mao immediately asked, "Where is the 10th Regiment now?"

The 10th Regiment, 4th Division, of the People's Naval Aviation, favored by Mao Zedong, had been reorganized from the 49th Regiment of the Chinese People's Volunteer Air Force, which had participated in the Korean War. In that war, this regiment had shot down 13 U.S. planes and damaged three others. Then, after the reorganization, it saw brilliant achievements in battles for national air defense. The regiment once set a record for combat in the stratosphere and shooting down high-altitude surveillance aircraft.

To counter the U.S. "sideswipe tactic," it was imperative to seize every moment when the U.S. was invading China's territorial airspace and shoot down the interlopers. Moreover, it was desirable that the

3. SAFEGUARDING SOVEREIGNTY

PLAN Aviation J-6 fighters

wreckage fall within the boundary lines of Chinese territorial waters. Considering the fact that at the time the U.S. aircraft greatly outperformed the Chinese planes, the aviation troops participating in air combat needed to have a perfect mastery of flying and fighting skills along with undaunted spirit. And so in 1965, the supreme commander, Chairman Mao, ordered the 10th Regiment, 4th Division, to be transferred to Hainan Island. They would be stationed there in battle array and wait for the U.S. aircraft to arrive.

The main aircraft type used by the U.S. for air reconnaissance was the BQM-34A "Firebee" unmanned high-altitude surveillance aircraft. The plane was small and lightweight, its flight speed was very fast, and it could fly as high as 66,000 feet. The plane flew by radio remote control. It was launched by transport aircraft and could be retrieved after missions.

To oppose the provocations of this unmanned high-altitude surveillance aircraft, the 10th Regiment formed a "Sharp Knife Squad" and waited in Haikou for the opportune moment to launch an assault. The Sharp Knife Squad was comprised of Squadron Commander Zhang Bingxian, Deputy Commander Shu Jicheng and Squadron Leader Wang Xiangyi, all of whom were master pilots.

While it was discovered that the advantages of the U.S. unmanned surveillance aircraft were their high-altitude flying capability and small size, it was also realized that their Achilles' heel was the need to fly according to preset programs.

The plane couldn't adjust to changing circumstances, and it couldn't fight back if attacked. But the flying altitude of the 10th Regiment J-6 fighters was not high enough to shoot down the unmanned planes. The zoom altitude of the U.S. aircraft was from 61,000 to 66,000 feet. By contrast, the operating altitude of the J-6 Fighter was only 57,000 to 59,000 feet. This relatively large altitude difference posed a major problem for the 10th Regiment during air battles.

China's pilots tried to remove bulletproof steel plates from the pilots' seats as well as machine guns, to reduce the weight of their fighters. But trial flights showed that the flying altitude of the fighters was still insufficient. Was it possible to use special methods to enable the J-6 to reach operating altitude and then continue to climb? The pilots of the "Sharp Knife Squad" had an idea, but it was too bold, because when fighters fly to the ultimate altitude and continue to climb, any pilot error or carelessness in operation can send them into a downward spiral. (The air becomes rather thin at high altitudes. And when air buoyancy is low,

The USN UAV BQM-34A "Firebee"

3. SAFEGUARDING SOVEREIGNTY

fighters will crash due to strong recoil from firing. The thin air cannot support their weight.)

After several daring trial flights, though, the pilots learned that if they could grasp the most suitable moment for pull-up, they could make use of an extremely brief flying altitude gained over peak altitude, to fly the J-6 to over 59,000 feet. Still, the problems at such an altitude were that the fighter was unstable, and it was rather difficult to aim and fire the guns.

According to Wang Xiangyi's memoir, "then my comrades did military exercises repeatedly in the air. We even suspended model airplanes from wires at the foot of our beds. We thought carefully about the whole process..."

On March 24, 1965, an U.S. unmanned air reconnaissance aircraft appeared, and Wang Xiangyi took off for a single sortie. It was time to test the new fighting tactic.

He found his target when it was 19 miles away. He corrected his course while climbing. When he was 2.4 miles from the U.S. aircraft, he immediately pulled up. When there was a quarter-mile between him and the U.S. plane, he fired two guns at once. The left wing of the U.S. aircraft was hit and smoke rose from it.

Wang Xiangyi followed hard after the U.S. plane and fired again. This time the latter fell straight down into the sea. The Sharp Knife Squad had won its first battle.

On March 31, 1965, another U.S. aircraft appeared. Shu Jicheng was ordered to intercept. (Wang Xiangyi took off later and was standing by.) Shu Jicheng found the U.S. aircraft when it was 20 miles away. Under guidance from the ground, he wasted no time in zooming at the limiting altitude to make close contact with the U.S. aircraft. To hit his target, Shu Jicheng waited to fire until there was but 360 feet between him and the U.S. aircraft, which was shot down and plummeted to the north of Sanya, Hainan Province.

On August 21, 1965, a U.S. drone first made a feigned flight toward the north of Vietnam then turned suddenly to the right and flew to Hainan Island. Shu Jicheng took off at once to intercept. When he was very close, he pulled up and fired a first round, but the target wasn't hit. So

Combat hero Shu Jicheng

he decided to come in close and fire again. This time, in but a minute the U.S. aircraft was in flames and falling. At this point there was less than 200 feet between the two planes.

In all, in less than half a year the 10th Regiment shot down three U.S. unmanned high-altitude surveillance aircraft. In December 1965, the honorary title "Eagle Regiment of Naval Aviation" was conferred on the regiment by the Defense Ministry.

EIGHT TO ZERO

While sending out unmanned high-altitude surveillance aircraft to harass Hainan Island, the U.S. Navy was also dispatching various kinds of manned fighters to invade the territorial air space over Hainan. The pilots continued to resort to the "sideswipe": they would enter Chinese territorial airspace for a moment and fly out over the high seas the next. People's Naval Aviation pilots tackled such provocation shrewdly.

On April 9, 1965, two groups of U.S. F-4B Phantom fighters took to the skies. The first group of four approached Yinggehai on Hainan Island, while the second invaded the sky above the Yellow Sea, Ledong County and other places. The F-4B Phantom is a type of high-speed shipborne aircraft. It carries four Sea Sparrow missiles, which can be launched under any meteorological conditions.

PLAN Aviation aircraft were ordered to take off and "patrol and monitor the activities of the U.S. fighters." In fact, the goal was to keep the fighters off the boundary line of China's territorial waters and effectively counter the "sideswipe" tactic.

The squadron commander for PLAN Aviation, Gu Dehe, led four J-5s, which took positions so as to meet the U.S. planes head-on. But by this time the U.S. fighters had already flown away. Meanwhile, the second group of four U.S. fighters took advantage of the occasion to invade China's airspace.

The PLAN flight formation was ordered to turn and pursue the invaders.

"Enemy spotted below, to the rear, at 3,300 feet!" reported the pilot of J-5 fighter 4, Li Dayun.

In the meantime, Gu Dehe had discovered that two U.S. fighters were flying to the left front of fighter 4. Li Dayun responded by making a sudden turn and forcing the U.S. fighters in the rear to rush forward. Then he made an anti-stern attack on one of the fighters and approached until there was only 200 yards between the two planes. He asked for an order to attack.

Gu Dehe, keeping in mind that the sole mission was to repel the U.S. aircraft, ordered Li Dayun not to attack. Li Dayun obeyed, turning and rejoining his formation. Meanwhile, the

U.S. F-4B Phantoms

squadron leader of fighter 3, Wei Shouxin, also made a sharp turn to throw off the two tail-biting U.S. planes.

After this, the People's Navy Aviation formation closed up and headed toward Wuzhi Mountain.

The U.S. fighters took this as a sign timidity on the part of the PLA. They intruded into Chinese territorial air space again and came closer to the Chinese fighters.

Suddenly, the tail-warning device on J-5 fighter 4 sent out an alarm. Li Dayun turned to discover that two U.S. fighters were on his tail. He immediately made a sharp turn to the left, which forced one of the fighters to give persistent pursuit in order to fire at him. This skillful tactic forced his opponent into a side-side maneuver and an attempt to glide and flee. Li Dayun, for his part, then followed hard on the other fighter, which had come to assist and fired two Sparrow missiles at Li Dayun. Li Dayun turned sharply to evade.

When Gu Dehe learned that the U.S. fighters had fired missiles at his J-5s and that a group of U.S fighters, coming closer, had already intruded

Visiting the wreckage of U.S. aircraft

into Chinese airspace, he gave an order: "Hurry after the U.S. fighters!" Seeing that the situation had become unfavorable, the two U.S. fighters launched four more Sparrow missiles, but the heavily protected Chinese fighters rapidly evaded and flew out of missile range.

The four U.S. missiles exploded in the air 650 to 1,300 feet from the Chinese fighter formation. After firing the missiles, the two U.S. fighters turned away from each other. J-5 fighters 3 and 4 rushed toward one of the two and forced it to flee at high speed.

At this moment, considering meteorological changes and the low-fuel situation of the J-5s, the formation was ordered back to base.

In this air battle, without firing a shot People's Navy Aviation not only broke the U.S. harassment pattern but also forced them to taste the bitter fruits of their own missiles.

Since the U.S. fighters had launched missiles in attack mode, Chairman Mao and Premier Zhou Enlai instructed that their former order, not to take the initiative in attacking U.S. aircraft, was no longer suitable to the new situation. From then on, China's policy on U.S. fighters' intrusion into her airspace would be "vigorously combat."

In June 1967, PLAN Aviation downed a U.S. F-4C fighter in the skies above Ling Shui County, in Hainan Province.

In February 1968, PLAN Aviation shot down one plane and damaged a U.S. Navy A-1H shipborne attacker in the skies above Wan Ning City, in Hainan Province.

Between 1965 and 1968, PLAN Aviation shot down and damaged eight U.S. aircraft of various types and suffered no casualties.

REUNION OF AIR RIVALS

Coming out of the air battles between the Chinese and the United States above Hainan Island, a legendary story is told. It arose from the war, but it transcends war.

At about 10:00 a.m. on September 20, 1965, Gao Xiang, captain in the Navy Aviation 10th Brigade stationed at Haikou airport, and deputy captain Huang Fengsheng were on standby duty when they received

Gao Xiang (right) and Huang Fengsheng

orders to intercept a U.S. Air Force craft flying from Da Nang in Vietnam to Leizhou Peninsula in China. Gao Xiang told the officers in a briefing, "Accept all, no return!" At 10:58 a.m., the signal for takeoff was given and two J-6 fighters took off to meet the U.S plane.

Under ground command guidance, Gao Xiang and Huang Fengsheng took to the skies to confront the U.S aircraft, which was turning to fly across the Leizhou Peninsula. Gao and Huang made an immediate 180-degree turn to intercept. The two J-6 fighters flew in formation and discarded their auxiliary tanks. They leveled off at 33,000 feet and approached the U.S aircraft, as instructed from the ground.

At 11:31 a.m., Gao discovered the U.S. aircraft seven miles away. He reported, "Discovered target at seven miles to the left front!" The command gave the order, "Target turned right. Cut-off attack! Approach and fire! Fire!"

The judgment of the command post was the same as that of the pilots. Gao Xiang executed a cut-off attack without hesitation. This was a movement fraught with great risk because the flying speed of the U.S. aircraft was greater and its flying radius larger. If Gao Xiang overdid

3. SAFEGUARDING SOVEREIGNTY

the cut-off maneuver, his fighter could be bitten in the rear by the U.S. aircraft. And if the cut-off was inadequate, the J-6 might be thrown off and lose the chance to fight. But Gao Xiang in fact flew perfectly to an advantageous attack position, trapping the U.S. plane with varying circular maneuvers.

Meanwhile, there was only three-quarters of a mile between the two planes. Gao Xiang closely pursued the U.S. aircraft, closing in bit by bit. At 1,000 feet he fired three rounds at his opponent, and he continued to fire until there was only 125 feet between the two aircraft. Later, his action in air combat would be described "bayonet fighting in the air."

On seeing the U.S aircraft bombing, Gao Xiang operated the pull rod and let it loose. Meanwhile, his fighter began to shake violently, and the right engine failed. It turned out that he had been hit by pieces of the exploding U.S. aircraft, as the two were very close. After returning safely to his airport, Gao Xiang counted 13 damage points on his plane, on the engine, flaps, nose and wing covering.

Having been hit, the U.S. plane, an F-104C Star fighter manufactured by the U.S.-based Lockheed Martin, dropped into the territorial waters of northeast Haikou. The flight speed of this aircraft could reach 1,500 mph, and the flying altitude exceeded 65,000 feet. The aircraft could carry four air-to-air missiles as well as aerial cannons. It could perform the double mission of tactical bombing and air combat. The plane was one of the state-of-the-art fighters in the 1960s, and this was the first time this aircraft had been shot down.

With his work in this air battle, Gao Xiang broke several records, enough for him to be written into the annals of world air combat history: for shooting down a second-generation U.S. supersonic aircraft with a first-generation China-made supersonic J-6; and for firing from between 125 and 1,000 feet, the smallest distance in air fighting since the start of the Jet Age.

The experienced U.S. pilot Philip Smith jumped from his

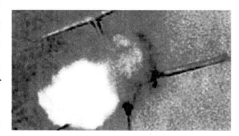
The explosion of an F-104C fighter

aircraft just before it exploded. The dazed pilot was nearly engulfed by seawater, which revived him. At that moment, a bamboo raft came into sight bearing an old man with yellow skin and black eyes who looked to him like a fisherman.

The pilot's first reaction was to raise his hands and give up his pistol. He then took from his uniform a 12 × 20-inch piece of white silk, a life-saving card written in 13 languages and issued by the Pentagon to U.S. soldiers during the Vietnam War. The words on the fabric were a request for help and a promise that the U.S. government would reward anybody who saved a U.S. soldier. The old Chinese man rescued Smith from the water and sent him under guard to where local troops were stationed.

"Firing at such close distance! Fearsome. Horrible," said Smith, who was still shuddering a few minutes before correspondents from the Xinhua News Agency came to take pictures.

Afterward, Smith received humane treatment, for which he was grateful. Not only could he have Western food, but he could write to his family and participate in sports. These things surprised him.

More surprises awaited. In 1971, during a secret trip to China by Henry Kissinger which marked a reconciliation between China and the United

The reunion of Gao Xiang and Philip Smith

States, the fates of Philip Smith and several other U.S. prisoners were taken into consideration among the topics the two nations discussed. In early 1973, after the United States had left Vietnam, China met its commitment and released Smith.

Then in October 1989, Philip Smith, then a businessman, took a trip to China, where he was able to meet his old rival Gao Xiang at the Jinjiang Hotel in Shanghai. He learned that Gao Xiang liked stamp collecting and inscribed a "Souvenir Envelope of the U.S. Navy Warships' First Visit to Shanghai" for him. Gao Xiang wrote on the back of a picture of him and Smith, "Two rivals in the air battle above the coconut trees in days of yore. Good friends shaking hands now at the Jinjiang Hotel."

In a relaxed and jovial mood, the two former rivals spoke that day for more than two hours about everything from career to family life. At the end of the conversation, Smith asked Gao Xiang, "Did you ever think that we'd have a reunion?" Gao Xiang said no. Smith said with emotion, "It was unthinkable in 1965. But times aren't what they used to be. I sincerely hope that the friendship between China and the United States, as well as between their peoples, will last forever."

Battle of the Paracel Islands

Over 180 nautical miles southeast of China's Hainan Island, in the vast expanse of blue water there, lie islands like star-shaped lotus flowers and pearls. These are the mysterious Paracel Islands, comprised of the Crescent group (Yong Le Islands) and the Amphitrite group (Xuan De Islands). These coral islands cover more than 200,000 square miles.

According to ancient records, as far back as the Qin-Han dynasties the ancient Chinese had been navigating the South China Sea and sailing among the islands there. They were the first to discover and name the islands and reef shoals. It was as early as the Qin Dynasty (B.C.E. 221–206) that China's government managed the Paracel Islands. From the Tang Dynasty onward (618–907), more and more Chinese started to ship and fish in the area. Later Chinese dynasties all took measures to administer and manage the islands. In the fifteenth century, when the outstanding Ming Dynasty navigator Zheng He led his fleet west, he passed the Spratly Islands and the Paracel Islands many times and anchored at some of the islands and islets. The Chinese names for the Crescent Group and the Amphitrite Group, Yong Le Islands and Xuan De Islands, were derived from the titles of the then-reigning Ming Dynasty emperors.

Also, according to archaeological discoveries, there was a settlement during the Tang and Song dynasties on Robert Island (Gan Quan Island) in the Paracel group. A lot of chinaware, iron pot debris and the remains of other produced goods and articles for daily use during those dynasties were excavated. This shows that, at least from the time of these two dynasties, Chinese people were living and producing things in the Paracel Islands. Until the Ming and Qing dynasties, many traces of their activity on the islands and islets of the Paracel group were being found. Also, on several major islands the remains of 14 ancient temples, built by Chinese fishermen, were discovered. Many stone tablets from the Qing dynasty and the period of the Republic of China were unearthed here as well.

During the 1970s, however, the indisputable sovereign right of China over the Paracel Islands was challenged by naked provocation. . . .

CRITICAL MILITARY POSTURE

In the afternoon of January 15, 1972, in Zhanjiang City, Guangdong Province, the intelligence office of the Command of the SSF received an especially urgent telegram. The cipher clerk decoded the message without delay, and, after reading it, the staff officer on duty, Li Zhaoxin, at once sounded an alarm at the Command Office. Momentarily, fleet commander-in-chief Zhang Yuanpei brought his chief-of-staff and other officers to the intelligence office.

The telegram came from militiamen from the Paracel's Robert Island (Gan Quan Island). It read, "At 1:20 p.m. on January 15, South Vietnamese warships rampantly bombed the national flag of the PRC on Robert Island."

3. SAFEGUARDING SOVEREIGNTY

The combat forces of the SSF working out a campaign plan

Actually, earlier that day the Command had received another piece of intelligence, that the South Vietnamese destroyers Lý Thường Kiệt (HQ-16) and Trán Bình Trong (HQ-5) had harassed and threatened two Chinese fishing boats in the waters near Robert Island. Several hours after this, the provocation by the South Vietnamese Navy escalated.

Many times before, South Vietnam had sent aircraft and ships to invade Chinese territorial waters and territory. They had already secretly replaced some sovereign signs of China and dispatched troops to occupy several islets and coral islands in the Spratly Islands. Now, after considering the activities of the South Vietnamese Navy (SVN), which had deployed landing troops to Da Nang, and after brief discussion and analysis, the officers in the Command decided that the South Vietnamese Government was in fact attempting to invade and occupy all of the Paracel Islands.

When it withdrew from South Vietnam, the United States left a lot of equipment and weapons to president Nguyen Van Thieu. But this enhancement of the nation's military strength did nothing to help the aggravating social contradictions in South Vietnam. Under the increasing pressure being imposed by the Viet Cong in the north, how could Nguyen Van Thieu deal with the island situation? His targets were the Spratly Islands and the Paracel Islands, and his choice seemed easy. Over 550 nautical miles from Hainan Island, the Spratly Islands were beyond the Chinese Navy's grasp at the time. On the other hand, although the Paracel Islands group was closer to Mainland China, Nguyen Van Thieu was emboldened, having more than 10 U.S. warships and the more advanced equipment he had inherited.

Reports about the military provocations by South Vietnamese forces were immediately submitted to the highest decision makers in China: Premier of the State Council Zhou Enlai and the vice chairman of the CMC. Along with Ye Jianying, they discussed countermeasures. After getting a go-ahead from Chairman Mao, they decided to intensify patrols and take military measures so as to protect the Paracels. This was the last military operation decision made by Chairman Mao.

Soon the SSF received instructions from higher-ups ordering the "safeguarding of national independence and state sovereignty and a resolute fight against the provocations by the Saigon authority." The instructions also stressed that the SSF "Be sure to stick to the rule of principled fighting. Chinese warships and vessels will not be the first to shoot under any circumstances. But if the intruders attack, Chinese troops must fight back relentlessly."

Zhang Yuanpei gave the order at once: detach two submarine chasers, Numbers 271 and 274, to form a patrol fleet with the deputy commander of the Yulin Naval Base, Wei Mingsen, in the waters near the Paracel Islands and perform operations tasks.

This was a rather formidable task. Due to the location of the South China Sea, in the south-most part of China, and to various historical factors, the military hardware of the SSF was weak and disadvantaged. At that time, the NSF had four Anshan-class Soviet destroyers. The ESF had frigates taken from the KMT Navy as well as a number of domestically made torpedo boats and escort boats. By contrast, the SSF had only several old and outmoded frigates and escort boats of small tonnage.

3. SAFEGUARDING SOVEREIGNTY

Although there was an SSF frigate fleet of the highest combat effectiveness at Yulin Naval Base, as it happens all four frigates were either being overhauled or were out of order. The remaining escort and torpedo boats were of very small tonnage and limited voyage capability and couldn't be used for naval operations in off-lying sea. So the only ships available to Wei Mingsen were six Type 6604 submarine chasers. The naval officers and men chose the two chasers in the best condition and fitted them with the best equipment and weapons available from other boats. Submarine chasers 271 and 274 were thus created. For a submarine chaser, the firepower on the Type 6604 was relatively strong. But because of the boats' age and low level of automation, all crewmen were required to be on deck when they fired. This made the men vulnerable to artillery shells coming from enemy warships. Despite the name "submarine hunter," this vessel was more often used for routine patrols, protecting fishing and other such low-intensity tasks. It was not a combat warship for the front line, but, given the emergency situation, there was no choice but to use it.

STANDING READY IN BATTLE ARRAY

On the morning on January 17, 1972, SSF submarine chasers 271 and 274, led by Wei Mingsen, arrived at the Crescent group of islands. Practically at the same time, the South Vietnamese Navy deployed the *Trần Khánh Dư* (HQ-4) destroyer and sent troops to invade Robert Island (Gan Quan Island) and Money Island (Jin Yin Island). This destroyer was a U.S. Navy "Savage" class convoy destroyer with a displacement of 1,750 tons.

Chinese Navy submarine chaser 274 in the Battle of the Paracel Islands

At 4:00 p.m., the *Lý Thường Kiệt* (HQ-16) and the *Trần Khánh Dư* destroyers again provoked the Chinese fishing vessels near the Paracel Islands. The PLAN formation arrived just in time and sent out a warning. The South Vietnamese warships turned and left.

In the early morning of January 18, the *Trần Khánh Dư* and the *Lý Thường Kiệt* sailed at high speed to the waters near the Crescent group and provoked fishing boat 407. They rammed and damaged this boat and hooked the iron grating of its bridge. At the arrival of the PLAN formation, the destroyers reluctantly released the fishing vessel.

At 4:10 p.m., the SVN sent the destroyer *Trần Bình Trọng* (HQ-5) and frigate *Nhật Tảo* (HQ-10) to the area near the Crescent group (Yong Le Islands). They sailed in a wedge-shaped formation along with the *Trần Khánh Dư*, a destroyer from Pattle Island, and approached the PLAN's Number 271. At this juncture, the Chinese formation reported the enemy status to Command, which alerted the front lines to stand ready for battle. The PLAN formation immediately weighed anchor and made sure their gun muzzles were in the right place. All the submarine chasers were about to meet and attack the advancing enemy at full speed. Seeing that the situation was turning unfavorable, the South Vietnamese vessels turned back and hid behind Pattle Island.

However, the SVN began deploying more warships to the Paracel Islands. Two PLAN submarine chasers encountered four South Vietnamese vessels with tonnages four times as large as their own. This was a most unfavorable situation. After discussing things with others at Command, Zhang Yuanpei decided to deploy more warships to the Paracel Islands. Submarine chasers 281 and 282 were soon mobilized to Woody Island (Yong Xing Island) for standby. And he immediately dispatched minesweepers 396 and 389 to the Paracel Islands to tackle emergencies near the Crescent group (Yong Le Islands).

After nightfall, the sea area near the Paracel Islands seemed to quiet down.

At 5:47 on January 19, the SVN destroyers *Trần Khánh Dư* and *Trần Bình Trọng* appeared in the open seas south of Antelope Reef, moving toward Duncan Island and Palm Island.

Then the destroyer *Lý Thường Kiệt* and the frigate *Nhật Tảo* also

3. SAFEGUARDING SOVEREIGNTY

appeared to the north of Palm Island and were approaching the PLAN's anchoring area.

After the *Trần Khánh Dư* and *Trần Bình Trọng* anchored one-third of a mile from Duncan Island, dozens of South Vietnamese soldiers with loaded guns used rubber boats to approach Duncan and Palm islands in stealth.

Zhang Yuanpei immediately ordered minesweepers 396 and 389 to the northwest of Palm Island to intercept the Lý Thường Kiệt and the *Nhật Tảo*. He also ordered submarine chasers 271 and 274 to the southeast of Palm Island to monitor the activity of the destroyers *Trần Khánh Dư* and *Trần Bình Trọng*.

After these deployments, Zhang Yuanpei took a good look at the friend-or-foe situation map in the combat room and remarked, "It's time for the new China's People's Navy to fight the foreign troops!"

A TRIUMPH OF FIGHTING BACK

Dozens of South Vietnamese soldiers began a landing operation. Some saw the PLA Army soldiers and militiamen on the island and shot at them. The PLA, however, being prepared for battle, immediately

Minesweeper 389 in forced landing after being damaged

launched a self-defensive counterattack. By means of a frontal attack on the South Vietnamese soldiers, they drove them back to their ships.

Although their landing had failed, the South Vietnamese naval forces, with their mighty warships and strong firepower, didn't take China seriously at all. At the moment, the fact was that the SVN was much stronger. With respect to equipment, the standard displacement of three SVN destroyers and one frigate ranged from 1,947 tons to 717 tons, for a total tonnage of over 6,600 tons. There were over 30 cannons of various calibers installed on board these vessels. In sharp contrast, in the Chinese Navy formation, the standard displacement of the minesweepers was 628 tons and that of the submarine chasers was only 332 tons. The total tonnage was 1,918 tons. And there were only 14 cannons on board the PLAN vessels.

The *Lý Thường Kiệt* sailed at full speed with its muzzle tilted high toward the formation that included PLAN's Number 396 and rammed the PLAN formation. During the ramming, the supports of the bridge, the railings on the port side and the minesweeping apparatus on Number 389 were severely damaged. At the critical moment, Number 396 was ordered to practice restraint and not fire first under any circumstances.

At 10:23, the *Trần Bình Trọng* rushed at high speed toward submarine chaser 274 and fired at its bridge. So the PLAN formation counterattacked. The flames of gunfire could be seen as the warships engaged in an intense battle.

To give full play to the maneuvering advantage of smaller boats, the PLAN formation fought at close quarters. Submarine chasers 271 and 274 attacked the *Trần Khánh Dư* and the *Trần Bình Trọng* while Numbers 396 and 389 attacked the *Lý Thường Kiệt* and the *Nhật Tảo*.

So the South Vietnamese tried to keep their distance from the Chinese formation, to be able to give full play to their own advantage of long-range artillery. But the PLAN vessels continued to pursue tightly and at full speed. In but a moment, the two sides formed a line-to-line combat state. The PLAN warships simultaneously fired small-caliber guns with high firing rate at the South Vietnamese warships. According to the memoir of the charge-man on ship 274, Li Ruyi (later awarded the first class merit distinction), during the battle he loaded 180 rounds

3. SAFEGUARDING SOVEREIGNTY   67

Ship gunners in battle

non-stop, which far exceeded his highest drill record. His hands were chafed so badly they were bleeding, but he wasn't conscious of the pain. Later he could see that all the shells he'd loaded were bloodstained.

Meanwhile submarine chaser 271 had identified the dead zone of the firing range of the *Trần Khánh Dư* and concentrated its fire on the bridge, which cut off communication. The ship's flags fell into the water. Finally, the ship fled to the open seas trailing flame and smoke.

Also meanwhile, submarine chasers 396 and 389 approached the *Lý Thường Kiệt* and concentrated fire on it. The SVN ship caught fire at many sites on the deck, and there were many explosions. At this time, the *Nhật Tảo* tried a surprise attack on Number 389. It was an extraordinary emergency, so two submarine chasers from the Number 281 formation moved to starboard of the *Nhật Tảo* and sprayed it with bullets and bombs. After a while, the ship was hit and caught fire.

China's submarine chaser 281 pursued the damaged *Nhật Tảo* relentlessly to keep it from escaping. When there was only 10 yards between the two ships, the PLAN soldiers rushed from their cabins and sprayed

The Five-Starred Red Flag streaming in the wind on recaptured Pattle Island (Shan Hu Island)

the soldiers on the SVN warship with machine gun and sub-machine gunfire. They also lobbed grenades at them.

The other SVN ships had never seen such a tactic and fled in confusion, leaving the severely damaged *Nhật Tảo* far behind. The submarine chaser then launched a violent attack on the lagging vessel at full speed and at close quarters. The frigate caught fire and exploded again, and at 2:52 p.m. it went down south of Antelope Reef.

Thousands of miles away in the SSF combat room, the ordinarily quiet and self-contained Zhang Yuanpei surprised everybody when in a loud voice he ordered that the spot where the *Nhật Tảo* had been sunk be marked forever. "This mark will tell the whole world that Chinese territorial waters, airspace and land are sacrosanct. If anybody dares to invade us, this will be his fate."

In high spirits, Zhang Yuanpei then ordered the Chinese warships and troops to attack on all fronts to eliminate totally the escaping enemy.

While this pursuit was taking place, however, he received an order from the Central Committee of the PLA via the Guangzhou Military

Region saying, "Withdraw the troops. Do not pursue the enemy. Sail back to the Paracel Islands to await orders." And so it happened that China exercised unilateral restraint so as not to escalate the battle. Soon the PLAN warships were back, as ordered.

Although the South Vietnamese naval forces had been routed, the defending troops on Pattle Island (Shan Hu Island), Robert Island (Gan Quan Island) and Money Island (Jin Yin Island) of the Paracels did not retreat. So at 9:00 on January 20, the Chinese Navy commenced landing operations to recapture the three islands. Actually, the South Vietnamese troops stationed on the three islands were already cornered like turtles in a jar and had no support from their navy. In only 10 minutes, the enemy on Robert Island laid down their arms and surrendered. Those on Pattle Island continued a stubborn resistance at a strategic position before the Chinese Navy launched an attack. After the Chinese troops took the beachhead, most of the enemy gave up all resistance and fled in disorder; some surrendered. The South Vietnamese troops on Money Island saw that Pattle Island and Robert Island had been recaptured and abandoned the island before being attacked.

The Five-Starred Red Flag was raised and fluttered in the wind once again over Pattle Island, Robert Island and Money Island.

This Battle of the Paracel Islands was the first time the PLAN conducted operations away from the continental coast. During this naval combat to guard their islands, the Chinese fought relentlessly, despite having outmoded and weak equipment and vessels. They used shrewd military tactics and were able to sink one SVN escort gunboat and damage three destroyers. Most importantly, they recaptured Pattle Island, Robert Island and Money Island. This was a just struggle to safeguard the sovereignty of China's territory and the first time since 1949 that the People's Navy had fought against foreign naval forces. Despite its small scale, this battle had far-reaching implications and will be ever remembered in the annals of history.

On June 21, 2012, the PRC established Sansha City. The seat of the municipal government of Sansha is on Yongxing Island, which administers the Xisha Islands, the Nansha Islands and the Zhongsha Islands.

CHAPTER 4

From Yellow to Blue Waters

ON THE LAST DAY of 1976, a Chinese Navy submarine surfaced in the Pacific Ocean. A group of young sailors rushed topside and shouted to the vast sea, "Pacific, here we are!"

The Chinese Navy had been working for nearly 30 years toward this exciting moment! To sail on the ocean had been the dream of several generations of Chinese Navy men. For a long time, due to the backwardness of the equipment, PLAN patrols could be done only near shore. But after decades of persistent effort, the People's Navy was able to move out from the yellow waters of the near shore to the deep blue waters of the ocean.

"An Expo of Various Outdated Vessels"

From the very start, the People's Navy's main source of weapons and equipment was confiscated old and damaged KMT vessels. The 183 warships and other vessels that had been surrendered, captured or discarded by the KMT Navy and other departments totaled 47,695 tons.

After liberating the coastal provinces and cities the People's Navy requisitioned and took over from their owners some commercial vessels and fishing boats. In all, the People's Navy took over 169 small- and medium-sized vessels whose overall dead weight was 71,501 tons.

The Navy also salvaged six shipwrecks, for another 1,890 tons, in the

Making a concerted effort to drag warships ashore for urgent repairs

middle and lower reaches of the Yangtze River and bought from Hong Kong 48 old vessels, totaling 28,076 tons.

Though the People's Navy owned some warships and other vessels, these were worn-out and backward in performance. The *Chutong*, bought from Japan at the end of the Qing Dynasty, was more than 40 years old. The *Yongji* had been built at the Jiangnan Shipyard at the end of Qing Dynasty and launched during the early days of the Republic of China. There were many vessels commissioned before and during the Second World War by the United States, the United Kingdom, Japan, France, Germany, Canada, the Netherlands and Australia. These were of all different types, and there were even 355 different kinds of main and auxiliary engines. Much of the equipment on the vessels was badly damaged, and many lacked accessories. The shipboard artilleries were from more than 30 countries, including the United States, the Soviet Union, the United Kingdom, Japan and France. Some of the vessels and warships weren't even equipped with guns. The shortage of instruments and related equipment was even more severe. Because of its various origins, the People's Navy was nicknamed "an Expo of Various Outdated Vessels."

The PLAN's having such a minimal number of fighting vessels was certainly not because of a lack of any great threats. At the time, in

4. FROM YELLOW TO BLUE WATERS

order to interfere with the development of the People's Navy, the KMT was continually sending aircraft for indiscriminate bombing runs that inflicted great losses on these vessels, a calamity for an already weakened People's Navy. The former KMT cruiser *Chongqing*, for one, was attacked by KMT heavy bombers. Twenty-two were wounded and six killed on the ship. There were many bullet holes in the body. In the end, the crewmen themselves sank their cruiser near Huludao Island harbor. Also, the vessels at anchor and being repaired provided more bombing targets for the KMT Air Force. During the KMT bombardment of the Shanghai Jiangnan Shipyard on January 25, 1950, 26 warships and other vessels were damaged.

With poor equipment and weapons, the Chinese Navy was not able to safeguard China's long coastline, never mind rank among the mightiest naval forces in the world. But the Navy had started from scratch from such foundations and was making solid progress one step at a time.

The Development of the People's Navy

Starting in the 1950s, the People's Navy blazed a trail through all manner of obstacles and was involved in an arduous undertaking. With China having a Cold War-oriented structure and being backward in science and technology and with an underdeveloped economy, the development of equipment and weapons was extremely difficult. But the Chinese Navy was committed to independent research combined with domestic manufacture using imports from abroad as templates. It was taking a path to developing equipment with Chinese characteristics.

REPAIRING THE OLD VESSELS AND WARSHIPS

Though described as an "Expo of Various Vessels from Ten Thousand Countries," the Chinese Navy cherished its hodgepodge of warships, considering them "treasures." Soon after its establishment, the PLAN first repaired many old and damaged vessels and refitted some merchant

Deng Zhaoxiang leading a crew repairing warships at the Dalian Shipyard

and fishing ships. The workers and engineers in the shipyards were also motivated by the PLAN. They risked their lives to repair and refit warships under the constant threat of bombardment by the KMT and in other extremely difficult circumstances. From September 1949 to May 1950, they repaired and refitted more than 130 vessels, to meet the needs of training and combat.

Aside from making repairs in shipyards, the East China Military Area Navy organized mobile repair stations in different regions. After the liberation of Zhou Shan, the front line was gradually moving south. On a small landing vessel equipped with lathe, drilling machine, electric welding and other equipment, dozens of technicians and soldiers carrying components patrolled and cruised everywhere around the Zhou Shan area. If they encountered Chinese vessels in trouble, they repaired them in a timely way, which greatly increased the latter's readiness ratio, although many were too severely damaged or outmoded to be saved.

Further, some of the requisitioned, dispatched and purchased ships were different from specially designed warships. Some were fishing boats. To refit these and make them combat-ready, it was imperative to equip them with guns and other battle accessories. At the time, one of the glaring problems was that it was rather difficult for a surface gun support to reach a horizontal standard, which might have an adverse

4. FROM YELLOW TO BLUE WATERS

effect on firing accuracy. To solve this problem, the Shanghai Shipyard experimented with a boring machine that did level cutting with a special steel frame cutter in the motor. Progress was slow, but this proved to be efficient in solving the problem of firing accuracy. In 1950, among the 123 warships in the East China Military Area Navy, as many as 799 vessels had been equipped with machine guns and shipborne guns. To transform fishing boats into warships was the first pioneer experience of the People's Navy.

IMPORTS

Refit and repair were not long-term solutions, though. To have a strong naval force it would be necessary to have in it fleet destroyers, frigates, submarines, minesweepers, submarine chasers, landing vessels, escort boats, torpedo boats and other kinds of combat vessels and warships. Auxiliary vessels were also required, including submarine tenders, training ships, repair ships, survey vessels, beacon working ships, salvage ships, underway replenishment ships and hospital ships. Also, all types

The first Soviet destroyer arriving at Qingdao

of weapons and mechanical devices needed to be fitted to the vessels. To meet such challenges, the Chinese Navy couldn't simply repair old vessels and refit commercial and fishing boats. It would have to manufacture domestically. But the nation was not strong at the time, the technology was backward and there was a critical shortage of professionals, so it was far too difficult to manufacture at home and independently in the short term. And so bringing in warships from abroad became another major way in which the People's Navy enriched its fleet in the early days.

In the first half of 1950, the situation was not at all bad, though. The Navy could buy some vessels, equipment and facilities from some Western countries through Hong Kong and from the Soviet Union. But by the second half of the year, due to the outbreak of the Korean War, western countries began to apply blockades and embargoes against China. Four frigates and four minesweepers ordered in Hong Kong in March were not delivered due to a ban by the British government. In early 1951, three minesweepers and four frigates on sale by businessmen in Hong Kong could not enter the harbors of Mainland China.

Therefore, the only alternative was to buy from the Soviet Union. Between 1953 and 1955 the People's Navy bought many weapons and much equipment from the Soviet Union, the majority of which were combat ships (both finished and semi-finished products), auxiliary vessels, all types of aircraft, special naval guns, underwater weapons, ammunition, special-purpose vehicles and equipment parts. Most of the warships were old. The four destroyers had started life between 1937 and 1941 and had been refitted or repaired before coming to China. The two C-type submarines received by the People's Navy at Lvshun were built in 1943, and by the time China got them they had already served for 10 years. Other C-type submarines had been launched in 1948. Some torpedo boats had been built during the Second World War.

Although the imported equipment and weapons did not meet expectations, they were much more professional than the worn-out warships and fishing boats the Navy had been using. By importing the equipment and boats, the People's Navy was able to establish combat fleets including destroyers, submarines, submarine chasers, torpedo boat fleets and

4. FROM YELLOW TO BLUE WATERS

aviation forces. These fleets helped the People's Navy break through the KMT naval blockades and liberate the coastal islands during the initial post-liberation period.

REFIT AND TRIAL MANUFACTURING

In 1952, the Chinese government negotiated with the Soviet Union for the purchase of a complete set of equipment, semi-finished instruments and technical materials. Afterward, the Chinese would assemble these parts and manufacture its own warships. Starting in 1953, China purchased technical drawings and the materials and equipment necessary to build five types of vessels: frigates, submarines, minesweepers, large submarine chasers and torpedo boats. For this, the People's Navy selected the Jiangnan Shipyard, Hudong Shipyard, Qiu Shipyard, Wuhu Shipyard and Wuchang Shipyard, which had the capability to manufacture the ships. These were expanded and technical improvements were made to them. Meanwhile, the Navy also decided to build a new shipyard, in Guangzhou, to do transferred manufacturing. In the second half of 1954, materials and instruments started to arrive at all these factories, and assembly and manufacturing were soon under way.

The task of assembling and manufacturing various combat warships in bulk was unprecedented in the history of Chinese shipping. The Wuhu Shipyard made 51 torpedo boats between February 1955 and 1959. After the first batch of imported materials and equipment for more than 20 torpedo boats had been assembled into finished boats, the Navy began to manufacture with materials

Mao Zedong on a China-made torpedo boat

produced domestically. After much R&D by engineers in the factories and by factory-posted military representatives, the difficulties were solved one by one, and the quality of the torpedo boats gradually improved. In 1958, the first torpedo boat made from domestic wood was tested, and the performance indices met the requirements. Altogether, 116 "transferred-manufactured" warships were made, and their tonnage totaled 47,400 tons.

Their fighting performance was up to the international standard between the late 1940s and the early 1950s, and the equipment and the warships were considerably advanced for the People's Navy at the time.

Still, even with the assistance of materials and technical designs from abroad, imitation was hard for a China with low productive capacity and backward technology, let alone the ability to make improvements to meet special circumstances. For instance, in building minesweepers the People's Navy encountered many difficulties. Before 1958, China had introduced two batches of materials and drawings for two Type-6610 Soviet minesweepers and for the trial manufacture of an underwater acoustics research ship. The factory them called Guangzhou Navy Factory 201, now the Guangzhou Huangpu Shipyard, was tasked with doing this. But the largest vessel built by this poorly equipped factory was a floating derrick of only 353 tons.

At the time, there was only a 17-ton crawler crane at this factory. And due to the position of the slipway, the crawler could move only along the starboard of the ship being constructed. So the derrick hands used their imagination and came up with a hand-made hanger rod to be used in combination with the crane. Finally, they managed to hoist the main and auxiliary engines just ahead of deadline.

The two minesweepers came into service in June 1960 after being refitted.

There are countless such stories from the early days of the People's Navy. Relying on science and with an independent and spirit of self-sufficiency, the Chinese did their best to catch up with the world. In making their progress, they showed great solidarity and tenacity and extraordinary wisdom. These are the traditions that the Chinese Navy will always cherish.

COPYING AND IMPROVING ON

In late 1950s, the development of PLAN weapons and equipment entered a period of copying transferred products. But the PLAN also built patrol boats, motor sailboats, landing boats and water tankers, despite China's shipbuilding industry being weak.

In addition, the PLAN developed and manufactured its own high-speed patrol boats, submarine chasers, frigates and other small vessels. The Naval Aviation Unit, too, grew stronger and equipped itself with domestic J-5 fighters, J-6 fighters and H-5 bombers. There were great advances as well in the technology of shore guns, antiaircraft guns and other equipment of the Navy Coastal Defense Unit. All this progress facilitated attacks to counter KMT harassment and the safeguarding of maritime security. And so the PLAN was able to win many sea battles, including the August Sixth Sea Battle and the Naval Battle to the East of Chong Wu.

On February 4, 1959, China signed an agreement with the Soviet Union to buy the design and manufacturing technologies and manufacturing rights for missile submarines, medium-size submarines, torpedo boats, hydrofoil torpedo boats, submarine-to-ground ballistic missiles and aerodynamic missiles. Fifty-one drawings and documents were involved. Among these vessels and warships, the Type-033 submarine was an advanced, conventionally powered sub designed in the mid-1950s, and improving on it opened the way for the PLAN to introduce equipment and technology on a large scale. In this manner, the technological level of the equipment of the People's Navy was improved greatly in just a short time.

CHINA'S OWN RESEARCH AND MANUFACTURING

Since the founding of the PRC, self-reliance has been a basic state policy. People in all areas of endeavor agree with the idea of "independent development," though every inch of progress has required tremendous effort.

The February 1957 maiden voyage of the PLAN's first China-made submarine

For the People's Navy, it was even harder to grow from what was an inherently weak foundation. During the 1950s and 1960s, in economic terms it was hard for the PRC to support updated equipment, and even if the country could afford updated equipment, purchasing opportunities were few. Further, although copying imported items and improving on them was useful, this would not be workable long-term. Chinese R&D and domestic manufacture was the only way to go. But this too was a path strewn with difficulties.

Throughout its history the KMT relied on purchasing and taking over second-hand and outmoded western warships combat vessels to build a naval force. For a long time there was neither scientific research strength nor allied industry effort in China. In such circumstances it was impossible to manufacture plates for ships, let alone entire warships.

In 1965, the PLAN set a goal to manufacture more advanced medium-sized surface warships, medium-sized submarines and nuclear-powered submarines. This marked three transitions in the history of the PLAN's development: from buying and copying foreign warships to making its own; moving from making small warships to making medium-sized ones; and shifting focus from guns to missiles as the weapons for surface warships.

In the 1970s, the PLAN researched and manufactured conventionally powered submarines, attack submarines, strategic nuclear submarines, destroyers, frigates, submarine chasers, antiship missiles, torpedoes and shore-to-ship missiles. The Naval Aviation fleet became equipped with aircraft equivalent to that of the Air Force. The ocean survey vessels displaced more than 11,000 tons, and there were salvage-and-rescue ships, rescue tugboats, comprehensive depot ships, mine layers, minesweepers and other service craft for maritime rescue, engineering, reconnoitering, transport, maintenance, medical care and other tasks. Thanks to this progress, in the 1960s the overall technological level of the PLAN's equipment and vessels rose to international levels. Deploying the new equipment, the PLAN won the battle of the Paracel Islands in 1974 and did convoy and surveillance work in the South Pacific.

Since the 1980s, the PLAN has been equipped with new-type guided missile destroyers, conventionally powered submarines, fighter-bombers, antisubmarine helicopters and other high-performance equipment and weapons. Earlier, the PLAN also researched and manufactured entirely new equipment with the latest technology, and the equipment and weapons of the Marine Corps and Navy Coastal Defense Units were greatly improved. The PLAN initially developed a modern equipment

Mao Zedong on the warship *Chang Jiang* in February 1953

framework to carry out maritime combat operations, base defense operations, sea-based self-defense nuclear counterattack with near-shore combat as a focus and operational and tactical maneuvers as a complement. During this period, in 1982, the first underwater missile was successfully launched from a submarine. Thus, by the early 1980s, the overall technological level of PLAN equipment had become competitive with that globally. The tactics and technological performance of the China-made naval equipment improved a great deal, too. Generalization, systemization and modularization were gradually realized. The main surface combat warships were greatly improved on in terms of being fitted with missiles, integration between command and control and implementation of stereoscopic combat zones.

In the 1990s, a new domestic conventionally powered PLAN submarine emerged. The Navy sent out second-generation destroyers and frigates to visit four countries in the Americas. The Naval Aviation Unit of the PLAN was equipped with the JH series of fighter-bombers. Comprehensive depot vessels displacing 11,000 tons sailed to the oceans. Many new missiles and electronic warfare systems were manufactured as main battle equipment.

Since the start of the twenty-first century, PLAN equipment development has progressed by leaps and bounds. Put into operation have been equipment and weapons of high IT levels, including a third generation of missile destroyers, frigates, submarines and combat aircraft, which have played a role in military exercises along with the new supporting equipment. One step at a time, automated command systems, satellite navigation systems, tactical software and other technologies have been applied to all kinds of warships, submarines and aircraft.

Meanwhile, between the 1990s and the early years of this century, the PLAN introduced some advanced technology and equipment from abroad. Latest-model destroyers, submarines and aircraft entered into service, accelerating the growth of the PLAN. Also, over the 60 years of PLAN development, the Navy completed a transformation from semi-mechanization to mechanization, and it is now undergoing informatization.

4. FROM YELLOW TO BLUE WATERS

CULTIVATING THE TALENT

In early May 1949, 555 defecting officers and sailors from the KMT Navy cruiser *Chongqing* (blown up by the KMT Air Force and later sunk near Hulu Island) arrived in Andong (now Dandong, Liaoning Province). After this, 74 more officers and sailors, from the warship *Lingfu* (recovered by the British and sold to Egypt), also arrived at Andong from Hong Kong. The CMC decided to establish the Andong Naval Academy.

This was the first school in the history of the PLAN. The vice president of the academy, Zhang Xuesi, was the son of Chinese warlord Zhang Zuolin and the younger brother of the famous KMT general Chang Hsüeh-liang (Zhang Xueliang). He secretly joined the CPC when he was 17 and at 24 became a commander at the front lines during the Anti-Japanese War. The political commissar Zhu Jun joined the revolution as early as the period of the Northern Expedition War (1926–1927) and had many legendary combat experiences. But the man who assumed the post of president of the new academy was not CPC but rather the former captain of the *Chongqing*, Deng Zhaoxiang.

Female cadets at the *Dalian* Naval College

Deng Zhaoxiang was an honors graduate of Greenwich Royal Naval College. He would later be appointed deputy commander of the PLAN and vice chairman of the Chinese People's Political Consultative Conference (CPPCC). He would serve in the Chinese Navy for more than 70 years and be witness to the three stages of development: under the Northern Warlord Government, under the National Government headed by Chiang Kai-shek, and under the aegis of the PRC. His military service would be the longest of all naval officers. There was no more suitable a man than Deng Zhaoxiang to be president of the PLAN's first academy. With him, a group of famous former KMT generals and officers participated in running the academy. This shows that the PLAN was eagerly seeking navy talent and valued its personnel a great deal. "To build a naval force, first build a school" was one of the fundamental principles in the development of the PLAN.

When the CMC appointed Zhang Xuesi vice president of the Andong Naval Academy, it also empowered him to establish a second formal naval college. In August 1949, the Military Commission sent him on a mission to the Soviet Union to observe and study. He was authorized to negotiate with the Russian consultants; he asked them to help China establish naval colleges. Zhang Xuesi visited several naval colleges in Moscow and St. Petersburg (then Leningrad) and reached an agreement with the Soviets.

In November 1949, the People's Navy established a naval college in Dalian using the Andong Naval College as a template. This was the first college to train and cultivate the main manpower for surface warships.

In August 1949, the East China Naval Force established the East China Naval Force Academy in Nanjing for the ideological and political education of former KMT Navy personnel and for technical training for Army personnel and newly arrived young intellectuals. Afterward, several colleges were established in Nanjing, Qingdao and elsewhere. After graduation, the cadres and trainees from these colleges were called up immediately to learn on the battlefield. These became the first fighting force during the early days of the PLAN.

By August 1957, the PLAN had command schools, machinery schools, submarine schools, speed boat schools, artillery schools, the First Avia-

4. FROM YELLOW TO BLUE WATERS

tion Academy of the Chinese Air Force, the Second Aviation Academy of the Chinese Air Force, the Unified Schools, political cadre schools, a logistics school and six other preparatory schools. There were also two college departments that laid a solid foundation for cultivating talented personnel for the Navy, namely, the naval department of the Military College and the naval engineering department of the Military Engineering College.

Over more than 60 years, the PLAN has established and improved on a college system in which the focus is on professional education and the relative separation between higher and professional education. In the meantime, in accordance with the policy of running large-scale and intensive schooling, the Navy also optimized the college structure and enhanced training efficiency.

Now there are eight People's Navy schools, including the PLA Naval Command College, the Naval University of Engineering, the PLA Naval Aeronautical Engineering Institute, the Dalian Naval Ship College, the Navy Submarine Institute, the Navy Land Warfare Institute, the Naval Aviation College and the Navy Officer College. These colleges and institutes have cultivated many talented personnel at various levels in the two major categories of naval command and engineering technology. They are also important bases for the Navy to carry out military studies and scientific and technological research.

Sailing the Oceans

For a long time, due to their backwardness and various technological levels, PLAN vessels could sail only in the near-shore yellow waters of the first island chain and were therefore nicknamed the "Yellow Water Fleet." Sailing the ocean was a long-cherished dream of PLAN servicemen.

December 31, 1976, was a significant date in the history of the PLAN. Submarine 252 cut through the blockade of the First Island Chain and entered the waters of the West Pacific. This was the first time the PLAN sailed the Pacific. On hearing this news from the captain, everybody on board was overtaken with joy. The director in charge of sonar issues kicked off his shoes in delight. When the submarine rose to the surface to be recharged, he threw the shoes into the sea and exclaimed, "This is a souvenir for the Pacific!" Other sailors who weren't on duty rushed to the deck and shouted to the vast ocean, "Pacific, hello! Pacific, here we are! Pacific, good to see you!"

Submarine 252 cruised in the Pacific underwater for 30 days and nights, for a voyage of over 3,200 nautical miles. This long voyage was a precious opportunity for enhancing the officers' and soldiers' navigational skills, for testing the performance of the China-made submarine and for opening up new routes for the Chinese Navy. The voyage was a landmark in the sailing history of the PLAN.

As China's overall national strength increased, the equipment and training levels of the PLAN have been greatly improved and its support capability during oceangoing voyage enhanced a great deal. The People's Navy finally broke through the first island chain blockade and set sail from the near-shore yellow waters to embrace the deep blue sea. This effort was to meet the demands of increasing international trade, to protect the interests of investors and to help safeguard world peace. It also ushered in a new era in the development of the PLAN.

Aboard the warship *Jinan*, former Chinese leader Deng Xiaoping said the Navy should not be defenders of a city. To develop the PLAN, he said China should "head for the world and face the oceans."

In early April 1980, PLAN's vessel 256 expanded its range and sailed into the vast Pacific, setting a new record for Chinese naval vessels on oceangoing voyages.

From April to July 1980, the Task Fleet—six destroyers, two supply vessels, two ocean salvage and rescue vessels, two ocean survey vessels and three ocean tugboats from the People's Navy, together with two measuring ships from the Commission of Science, Technology and Industry for National Defense, one tugboat from the Ministry of Transport and four helicopters—crossed the Equator and sailed to the South Pacific to be a maritime guard for the test launch of a long-range carrier rocket. The total round-trip voyage would be more than 8,000

4. FROM YELLOW TO BLUE WATERS

nautical miles without docking, an unprecedented feat for PLAN in terms of large-scale voyages.

Today, after decades of arduous development, the Chinese Navy can finally sail freely on the vast oceans. This is not a show of military prowess. Besides safeguarding national security, the increasingly powerful Navy has started to shoulder more international obligations and undertake peacekeeping missions.

On August 2, 1979, Deng Xiaoping inspects warship 105

In 1985, in fact, the Fleet Formation of the People's Navy started sailing to the continents on goodwill visits and began to participate in joint military exercises with warships from many countries. In 2002, the Fleet Formation of the People's Navy set sail for the first time on an around-the-world voyage.

Starting in December 2008, the group sailed to the area around Somalia and the Gulf of Aden to escort commercial ships and protect national maritime interests and world peace.

CHAPTER 5

Establishment of the PLAN

NEARLY ALL the commands at the different levels of the Chinese Navy are organized based on the corresponding entity of the Army. Therefore, the Navy is preserving the fine tradition of the Army while also embodying the technological characteristics of a naval force.

PLAN Headquarters

The Headquarters of the People's Navy was founded on April 14, 1950, having been reorganized from the Headquarters of the PLA 12th corps, its immediate troops and other units. The Navy includes the PLAN Command Headquarters, the Navy Political Department, the Navy Logistics Department and the Navy Equipment Department. These are all located in Beijing.

The Navy Command Headquarters is responsible for combat control, training, communications, military affairs and other work.

The Navy Political Department is responsible for propaganda and education, law and discipline, cadre management and mass work among other assignments.

The Navy Logistics Department is responsible for materials supply, health-care, financial affairs, naval bases, barracks management and other relevant work.

The Navy Equipment Department is in charge of the research for and manufacture and repair of all kinds of warships, aircraft, weapons and equipment.

The PLAN administers three fleets: the NSF, the ESF and the SSF. Directly under its jurisdiction there are naval colleges and academies, scientific research institutions, test bases and some immediate forces.

The PLAN's Three Fleets

THE NORTH SEA FLEET

The NSF is headquartered in Qingdao, in Shandong Province. Its defense areas include the Bohai Sea and the Yellow Sea. Under the NSF there are an Aviation Command, several bases and training bases and maritime garrison commands. Its equipment and weapons include destroyers, landing vessels, minesweepers, frigates (escort vessels), submarines, missile gunboats and support ship detachments or brigades.

In September 1950, the headquarters of the 11th Army of the PLA, along with the troops directly subordinate to it, were moved to Qingdao and reorganized into the Qingdao Naval Base, directly under the Military Commission of the Central Committee of the CPC and the People's Navy. In April 1955, after the withdrawal of the Soviet troops from Lvshun Military Port, the Railway Public Security Command and other bodies were reorganized into the Lvshun Naval Base, reporting to the CMC, in order to take over defense affairs and port facilities. The NSF was established at the Qingdao Naval Base. The Lvshun Naval Base was also included in the Fleet.

THE EAST SEA FLEET

The ESF command is headquartered at Ningbo, in Zhejiang Province. The Fleet defends the East Sea. In this Fleet there are Aviation Command, several bases and maritime garrison commands, destroyers,

5. ESTABLISHMENT OF THE PLAN

Destroyer formation of the East Sea Fleet

submarines, frigates (escort vessels), landing vessels, minesweepers, missile gunboats and support ship detachments or brigades.

The predecessor of the ESF was the East China Military Area Navy, the PLAN's earliest established naval force. The East China Military Area Navy was founded at Baima Temple on April 23, 1949, and initially organized from several headquarters of the training divisions of the Third Field Army of the PLA.

In October 1955, the East China Military Area Navy was reorganized into the ESF. The commands were stationed in Nanjing, Shanghai and elsewhere.

THE SOUTH SEA FLEET

The SSF is headquartered in Zhanjiang, in Guangdong Province. It defends the South Sea and is the largest of the three fleets. In the South Sea Fleet is the Aviation Command, and several naval bases and marine police regions are under the aegis of this fleet. Its equipment and weapons include destroyers, submarines, frigates (escort vessels), landing vessels, minesweepers, missile gunboats, support ship detachments or brigades and marine brigades.

The predecessor of the SSF was the River Defending Unit of the Guangdong Military Region. This comprised the Navy Takeover Unit of the Guangzhou Military Control Commission and a division of the Guangdong-Guangxi Column. In December 1950 it was reorganized as the SSF of the Central South Military Area.

In October 1955, the Central South Military Area became the SSF and was stationed in Guangzhou.

Five Branches of the PLAN

The units of the PLAN include five branches of armed forces including naval surface forces, submarine forces, air forces and a land army. It also consists of service support forces that specialize in reconnaissance, communication, inspection, engineering, navigation support, electronic information, hydrometeorology, rescue, chemical defense, logistics and supply and repair. Each branch of the military service is an indispensable part of the whole force and a cooperative naval operation.

NAVAL SURFACE VESSEL UNIT

The naval surface vessel unit fights on the surface and provides service support. Its can carry out continuous tactical operations at sea for long periods. It is not only the main force for offensive and defensive operations against all kinds of targets, it is also a significant force that provides all kinds of support to guarantee maritime operations. In the naval forces around the world, the naval surface vessel unit is generally the largest and its military strength the mightiest.

The elements of this force include aircraft carriers, battleships, cruisers, destroyers, frigates (escort vessels), missile gunboats, submarines, mine layers, minesweepers, landing vessels and all kinds of service support ships. The surface fleet is responsible for attacking and destroying enemy warships (ASUW) and transporting landing troops to enemy-controlled coastline, as well as for maritime surveillance, patrolling,

5. ESTABLISHMENT OF THE PLAN

SSF ship-against-ship confrontation exercise

antisubmarine warfare, mine warfare (MIW), minesweeping, merchant ship convoy protection, fishing grounds protection, search-and-rescue (SAR) missions, maritime medical care, maritime training, maritime surveying, navy weapons testing, maritime engineering, personnel transport and logistics.

The naval surface vessel unit is the oldest naval force. It has the most armed forces. It is also one of the key elements of a naval force. Around 1200 B.C.E., the earliest warships in recorded history came into use in Egypt, Phoenicia and Greece. At that time, people rowed with oars and rode the wind. The main tactics in sea battles were striking and on-board activity. Along with progress in our ability to produce ships and weapons and the rapid progress of science and technology, many branches of the armed forces arose to meet the need for strengthened maritime security. And so surface vessels began to play a rather significant role in maritime warfare.

In the eleventh century, the warships of the Northern Song Dynasty were already equipped with all kinds of firearms.

At the end of the fourteenth century, the French began equipping their warships with guns, the start of using guns on western naval forces warships.

In the nineteenth century, steam-powered warships came into use. From then until the beginning of World War II, large-warship warfare consisted of confrontations between guns and armor.

The naval surface vessel unit was also the earliest organized unit of the PLAN. In November 1949, the East China Military Area Navy established the first two of its fleets, the First Warship Fleet and the Second Warship Fleet. Later, the PLAN established many units, including torpedo speedboat, destroyer, submarine chaser, escort vessel, landing vessel, minesweeper, missile vessel and service support. Such units were usually organized into the three levels of detachment, group and squadron (for example, the Destroyer Detachment, the Escort Vessels Group and the Missile Speedboats Squadron).

Over 60 years of growth and progress, the Naval Surface Vessel Unit of the PLAN has become a significant maritime attack-and-support force consisting of various types of vessels equipped with modernized weapons and having considerable fighting ability.

SUBMARINE UNIT

The submarine unit is one of the PLAN's assault forces. The unit is responsible for raids against strategic underwater enemy targets, anti-submarine operations and maritime reconnaissance. It is also important for attacking enemy naval and coastal targets and pinning down the enemy. The submarine unit is highly self-sufficient and has great endurance and is able to conceal its activities. It can operate independently, but it can also conduct joint operations with aircraft and other warships.

The submarine unit contains both conventionally powered and nuclear- powered vessels. It has torpedo submarine forces, missile submarine forces and strategic missile submarine forces, depending on how the vessels are equipped. From underwater the submarine unit can launch torpedoes, mines and missiles. The force can annihilate large- and medium-sized transport vessels and warships, destroy enemy lines

5. ESTABLISHMENT OF THE PLAN

Submarine formation

of communication at sea, protect its own lines of communication and destroy enemy bases, ports and important targets on shore. The unit also does reconnaissance, mine laying, antisubmarine combat and patrolling, and it transports personnel and materials.

In 1775, American inventor David Bushnell made a small wooden submarine, "Turtle." This was the first submarine used in combat. After that, sea battle strategy developed to include underwater fighting, setting the stage for warships to engage in underwater battles.

From the late nineteenth century to World War II, submarines powered by diesel engines, motors and batteries gradually came on the scene. Then came torpedoes, guns, radar equipment, underwater acoustic equipment and other observation and communication equipment. The concealment ability, maneuverability and combat capabilities of submarines also improved a great deal. Thus, they became one of the main attack weapons of a naval force. During World War I, German submarines showed skill in battle and received great attention around the world. Submarines were then improved significantly during World War II, during which time their maneuverability and ability to hide were greatly improved and their weapons and technology significantly advanced. Submarines then sank many types of warships and vessels, including aircraft carriers and battleships, and showed great power.

Electricity was widely applied in submarines manufactured after

World War II. Then the installation of advanced nuclear-powered equipment in subs significantly improved underwater navigational speed and endurance. And the combat capabilities of submarines were further advanced, by leaps and bounds, with the installation of missiles and nuclear weapons.

During the initial phase of PLAN development, submarine units were established as a first priority. In April 1951, the PLAN formed a submarine training group of more than 270 men who were sent to the submarine unit of the Soviet Union Navy Pacific Fleet stationed in Lvshun Port. In August 1953, the Navy Submarine School, the Fourth Naval School of the PLAN, was established.

In July 1954, the PLAN took over four Soviet submarines to establish its first submarine troop: the Navy Independent Submarine Detachment. In October 1955, the Navy Independent Submarine Group was expanded into the Navy Submarine Division.

According to the June 4, 1953, agreement between China and the Soviet Union, the latter agreed to a compensated transfer to China of the right to build the Whiskey-class conventionally powered torpedo submarine (known in China as the Type 6603 submarine, or Type 03 for short). The first such sub was formally delivered to the submarine force in October 1957 and became the first type of submarine manufactured by China. This was the beginning of China's mass-producing subma-

A PLAN submarine on the surface

rines for the newly founded PRC. (Chairman Mao himself inspected a submarine.)

On February 4, 1959, the two parties concluded another agreement. Here, the Soviet Union agreed to a compensated transfer to China of the right to build the new Romeo-class conventional torpedo submarine (which China called the Type 033) and Golf-class conventionally powered ballistic missile (Type 031 in China).

In April 1974, the first Type 035 submarine was finished and delivered to the Navy. This marked for China a new stage in self-design and research on conventionally powered submarines.

In August 1974, China's first nuclear-powered attack submarine, the *Long March 1*, was formally incorporated into the PLAN's battle array. China was the fifth country to launch its own nuclear-powered sub. In 1981, the submarine set out on a nearly month-long voyage. In 1983, it went even farther. In February 1986, after dozens of days and nights of endurance testing, the Chinese nuclear missile and personnel were found to be competent.

In October 1982, China successfully carried out its first underwater test launch of a carrier rocket. In August 1983, China's first missile-bearing nuclear submarine came into service. In September 1988, the successful underwater launch of a ballistic missile by a nuclear submarine showed that the PLAN could provide underwater strategic deterrence and limited nuclear counterattack.

The organizational unit of the PLAN Submarine Unit is the division or the base, each of which contains several submarines.

NAVAL AVIATION UNIT

The Naval Aviation Unit is a branch of the navy that mainly carries out combat tasks at sea and in coastal airspace, with naval aircraft the main equipment. It is the main force for the PLAN for seizing air supremacy above the sea. Its highly mobile operational capability and great assault capability make it possible for the naval aviation force to carry out various offensive and defensive combat and guard tasks.

On January 26, 1911, the seaplane, invented by the American Glenn Curtiss, made a successful test flight. In July of the same year, the U.S. Navy purchased the seaplane, making it the first country to bring the seaplane into formal service.

Two J-8 fighters cruising above Hainan Island

Later, with the advent of the aircraft carrier, carrier-borne aviation came into play. During the two world wars, naval aviation made great strides. In the Pacific War, China' Navy Aviation Unit was sometimes the only Chinese troop fighting.

In the early days of the PRC, the PLAN began to develop a naval aviation force that could deal with the threats of the KMT against the mainland at sea and from the sky. In October 1950, a navy aviation school was established at Cangkou Airport, in Qingdao, and this marked the start of navy aviation in China.

In June 1952, the First Division of Navy Aviation was formed at Shanghai's Hongqiao Airport. It was soon equipped with Soviet-made Tupolev T-2 torpedo bombers and Lavochkin La-9 fighters. That same year, the leading agency of the Naval Aviation Unit was established at the order of the CMC of the PLA (In October 1955, it was renamed the Naval Aviation Military Department. In November 2003, it was eliminated and the troops were incorporated into related fleets and command headquarters). At that time, the organization was complete and included leading agencies, aviation forces and schools. The Navy commemorates September 6 as the founding day of Navy Aviation. It is the only one of the five Navy branches to have a founding day distinction.

Afterward, the PLAN Aviation Unit bought some planes and various pieces of equipment from the Soviets and took over some from the Air Force. Before 1955, six aviation divisions, two independent regiments, eight regiments of antiaircraft guns, radar troops and other antiaircraft forces had been formed. There were several hundred planes of various types. The Navy's aviation unit was taking shape.

From the start, the Naval Aviation Unit largely grew and developed via battle. At 2:00 p.m. on March 18, 1954, patrol boats around Sanmen Bay, Zhejiang Province, were attacked by six KMT Navy aircraft. Two PLAN vessels were damaged. On learning of this, the Naval Aviation Unit immediately dispatched two MiG-15s to the airspace above Nantian Island, and they shot down two KMT planes. This was the first air battle of the Naval Aviation Unit. In the combat and operations work to liberate the coastal islands, escort ships and fishing boats, in national air and naval base defense, in the War to Aid Vietnam and Resist U.S. Intervention, and in hundreds of other operations, aviation played an indispensable role. The Unit shot down and damaged more than 400 enemy aircraft in total.

The PLAN established the Naval Aviation Unit with a focus on shore-based aircraft. The force consists of bombers, fighter-bombers, fighters, strike aircraft, reconnaissance airplanes, seaplanes, helicopters, warning craft, electronic countermeasures craft, transport craft, rescue craft, support-task troops and antiaircraft forces. The force is organized into fleet aviation command, aviation division, regiment, group and squadron, antiaircraft missiles, antiaircraft guns, radar regiments, battalions and companies. Airports and other related support facilities were also specially built for Naval Aviation in coastal areas and on some islands.

The Naval Aviation Unit employs a combined system of aviation and ground-to-air defense. These days, Naval Aviation is a maritime attack-and-support force comprised of all kinds of shore-based aircraft, aircraft carriers and seaplanes, all of which have achieved preliminary modernization on a massive scale.

MARINE CORPS

The Marine Corps is the armed force mainly responsible for landing campaigns with basic equipment of amphibious combat weapons. It is the vanguard landing attack force, with strong firepower, high

The Marine Corps in a landing operation

maneuverability, fierce assault power and solid protecting power. It is also an important mobile combat force.

The earliest-known marine corps was formed in 1537 by the Spanish King Charles I. It fought side-by-side with the famous Spanish Armada. Later, Russia, the United States, Britain, France, Japan and other countries established their own marine corps. During the two world wars, the marine corps played an important role.

The earliest unit of the PLAN Marine Corps was established under the River Defending Unit of the Guangdong Military Region in December 1949. But the battalion didn't have landing operation capability. In April 1953, to liberate the southeast coastal islands occupied by the KMT Navy, the East China Military Region Navy formed the 1st Marine Regiment and the Amphibious Tank Instructing Regiment. In December 1954, these became the Marine Division, the first formal marine force in the PLAN. The division had combat landing capability and coastal defense maneuver combat capability. Later, it was reorganized into the garrison force of the Shanghai garrison command and given a change in mission. In May 1980, the Marine Corps was rebuilt at Hainan Island into an important ship-to-shore attack and coastal defense force of the Navy Joint Maneuver Formation.

5. ESTABLISHMENT OF THE PLAN

The need to rebuild the Marine Corps became urgent after the profound lessons learned in the landing on the Paracel Islands. In 1974, to recapture some of the Paracel island group, the Army units stationed at Hainan Island were temporarily detached to participate in a landing mission with the Navy. Due to a lack of the experience in sea-crossing assault landing operations, the officers and soldiers could hardly bear the motion of the rolling waves. They became seasick and vomited, and this struck a deadly blow to their ability to fight. So the Marine Corps was reorganized from the infantry and armored forces that participated in the Battle of the Paracel Islands.

The organizational units of the PLAN Marine Corps are marine brigade, regiment, battalion and company. There are infantry, armored force, artillery, engineer, anti-chemical warfare and amphibious reconnaissance troops, among other services. Over the 30 years of its development, the Marine Corps has done many jobs, including reef defense in the Spratly Islands, flood defense in 1998, the "Sharp Sword" maneuver, earthquake relief after the Wenchuan quake, ocean escort and other important missions. It has also been inspected over 40 times by China's military officers and by senior military leaders from more than 60 countries. In a word, the Marine Corps is playing an important role in safeguarding China's national security, protecting national interests and assisting in national economic development.

On October 1, 1999, the Marine Corps made its debut in the National Day Parade. The heroic posture and uniformity of movement impressed the world.

In August 2005, the Marine Corps participated in a joint maneuver with Russia, Peace Mission 2005. During this formal maneuver there was a 7 Bft wind at sea, and the waves

Marine Corps women on parade

were 10 feet high. Marine Corps soldiers skillfully drove an amphibious tank on the rolling waves. They were successful in the maneuver.

In the PLAN Marine Corps there is a female amphibious reconnaissance group. Dozens of young women are fully armed and wear ocean camouflage. They train alongside the men in shooting, overcoming obstacles, fighting, doing reconnaissance, swimming, climbing and parachute jumping. Some of the women practice Chinese kung fu and are experts at Shaolin boxing and traditional swordsmanship. Their fighting skills are in fact remarkable. Sometimes they're sent to deserted islands for wilderness survival exercises. There they have to dig wild vegetables, pick wild berries, catch snakes and rats and go fishing, so as to maintain physical strength. The women have been successful at many missions, including training, maneuvering and emergency and disaster relief, thus gaining fame as the "Amphibious Lady Warriors."

After watching the training of the Marine Corps of the Chinese Navy, U.S. Marine Corps commander General Gerard Kelley remarked, "You have good reason to be proud!"

COASTAL DEFENSE UNIT

The coastal defense force is charged with coastal defense and combat with shore guns and shore-to-ship missiles. The force is deployed in strategic positions along the coastal areas and on islands. The advantage of such a unit is its quick reaction ability. Its weapons are of wide range, high accuracy and great power. The positions are fortified and easy to hide. The ammunition reserves are adequate. The unit has strong battlefield survivability and can easily carry out wide-ranging firepower maneuvers. So this unit is important for attacking or repelling enemy invasions from the sea and by support vessels sailing near shore and for assisting island garrison forces.

In the B.C. era, some maritime countries had already developed coastal defense facilities and deployed armed forces to guard islands. Then, after their invention in the late fifteenth century, guns were soon installed on warships and in coastal batteries. These are considered the predecessor of the coastal defense force.

5. ESTABLISHMENT OF THE PLAN

Coastal Defense Unit in training

After the eighteenth century, many countries incorporated coastal defense forces into their navies, and these immediately played an important role in coastal defense campaigns. At that time, the firing range of coast artillery was within three nautical miles. Therefore, many countries stipulated that their territorial waters were within three nautical miles of their coasts. A host of coastal defense officers and soldiers sprang up over the history of modern war in China, including Chen Huacheng and Guan Tianpei, who heroically fought invading foreign vessels and sacrificed their lives in doing so.

The Coastal Defense Unit of the People's Navy was developed from coastal artillery troops. The Navy established the first Artillery School in August 1950 in Qingdao. Then on October 21, the first coastal artillery battalion was established in Qingdao, and this marked the birth of the Coastal Defense Unit. The unit's equipment included army guns on loan and 130mm and 100mm caliber guns purchased from the Soviet Union. Later, search lamps and distance gauge equipment also came into use. By October 1952, the Coastal Defense Unit of the People's Navy had deployed 99 guns along the coast. By 1955, there were 19 regiments in the Coastal Defense Unit posted all over the coastal areas and on some islands off Mainland China.

In 1959, the PLAN launched the first shore-to-ship missile. The former CCCPC chairman Zhu De, vice chairman Dong Biwu and many other state leaders and high-ranking officers were present for the launch. It was a grand and spectacular event.

In the same year, the Navy decided to reorganize the artillery school into a college, aiming to cultivate a specialist group for missile engineering technology and to offer various majors related to missile engineering technology. In 1963, the Coastal Missile Group was established on an NSF base. In 1967, the first Coastal Defense Missile Battalion, equipped with missiles manufactured by China, joined the Navy combat personnel. The establishment and development of the Coastal Defense Missile Force greatly expanded the combat range of the PLAN's coastal defense force.

For over 60 years, China's Navy Coastal Defense Unit has contributed greatly to combat, including at the battle of the bombardment of Jinmen Island and at several other battles to liberate and safeguard the southeast coastal islands. In 1955, two coastal defense companies of the PLAN participated in the Battle of the YiJiangshan Islands. The gun company deployed on Toumen Mountain destroyed enemy artillery positions and effectively supported the landing forces. In the battle of bombarding Jinmen Island in 1958, more than 10 shore defense companies took part and brought into full play the advantages of a coast artillery of wide range and great firepower. They not only sank or damaged many KMT combat vessels and warships and destroyed a number of enemy positions, they also inflicted heavy losses on the KMT Navy Command in Kinmen (Quemoy).

The Coastal Defense Unit of the PLAN includes coastal missile forces and coastal artillery forces. The organizational units of the Navy Coastal Defense Unit include coastal artillery, shore-to-ship missile regiment, battalion, company and so on. The unit is equipped with all kinds of shore-to-ship missiles and automated guns of different caliber. They not only wage close combat and destroy relatively small maritime targets, they can also accurately attack large- and medium-sized targets at distances. In a nutshell, the unit has become an important armed force for defending naval bases and strategic coastal locations.

CHAPTER 6

The PLAN's Main Weaponry and Equipment

A NAVY (also called a maritime force) is a comprehensive armed force. To be able to participate in all kinds of combat and perform diverse tasks, the PLAN is equipped with various types of surface vessels, submarines, aircraft, missiles, artillery, tanks, armored vehicles, radar and other equipment and weapons.

Naval Vessels

The large- and medium-sized naval surface vessels of the Chinese Navy bear both pennant numbers and ships' names. The small boats have only pennant numbers. Many of the vessels of the Chinese Navy are named after cities, indicating their relationships to cultural backgrounds. Ships' captains and mayors (county magistrates) visit each other often and do various kinds of "support the army and cherish the people" activities to promote the construction of ships and the development of cities. China has also held "Warships and Cities Forums" in the birthplace of the Chinese Navy, Tai Zhou, and in other places, and the forums are a major feature of the cultural development of the Chinese Navy.

DESTROYERS: FROM THE BIG FOUR TO CHINESE SHIELD

A destroyer's primary weapons are missiles, torpedoes and shipborne guns. This is a medium-sized warship that can carry out multipurpose operations. At any given time it can be tasked with antiaircraft defense, antisubmarine warfare, convoy work, patrolling, surveillance, blockading, salvage-and-rescue operations, shoreward attack, combat support and other missions. Modern destroyers displace from 3,300 to over 8,800 tons. Their navigational speed is in excess of 30 knots.

The earliest destroyers emerged in the late nineteenth century. The British Navy used them to attack torpedo boats. They displaced only 265 tons. With the growing demands of sea battles and progress in science and technology, destroyer displacements became larger and their functions increasingly versatile. They have gradually become an important type of warship in naval forces around the world. In the 1950s, destroyers began to be equipped with missiles, and various equipment and instruments were also improved. The installation of helicopters on destroyers strengthened the antisubmarine warfare and other combat capabilities.

Modern-grade destroyer: the *Ningbo*

6. THE PLAN'S MAIN WEAPONRY AND EQUIPMENT

The earliest introduction of destroyers into the PLAN was in October 1954 and July 1955. The four Soviet Type-07 destroyers were called the Big Four. At the time, these were the largest of the PLAN's main force warships. (They're all decommissioned now.) One of these four destroyers, the *An Shan*, which witnessed the early growth of the PLAN's combat fleet, is now anchored at the Qingdao Naval Museum. Its standard displacement is 2,396 tons, and its cruising speed is 18 knots. Its main weapons are 130mm and 37mm guns. It was also fitted with missiles.

The Type-051 destroyer was the first destroyer made in China. It was also the first PLAN warship with ocean combat capability. This destroyer came into service in 1971. Later, many versions of an improved Type-051 destroyer emerged, with various capabilities, displacements and updated weapons.

The Type-052 is a new type of China-made destroyer. Several units of the PLAN were recently equipped with this destroyer. The Type-052 has strong antiaircraft, antiship and electronic combat capabilities. And so it has gained fame as the "Chinese Shield."

The modern-grade destroyer was introduced from Russia in two batches after 2000. Its strong antiaircraft and antiship combat capability is conducive to promoting the PLAN's ocean-fighting ability. Destroyers have become the PLAN's main warships.

FRIGATES: THE PLAN'S MAIN SHIPS

Frigates are small- and medium-sized warships equipped with missiles, shipborne guns and torpedoes as their main weapons. This type warship is the most commonly and extensively used vessel in navies around the world. It can do convoy work, patrolling, surveillance, antiaircraft operations, antisubmarine operations, antiship operations, coastal attacks, landing support and other tasks. The modern frigate displaces 660 to 5,500 tons, and its navigational speed ranges from 24 to 32 knots.

During the sixteenth and seventeenth centuries, the Spanish and Portuguese navies used three-masted warships as frigates. In the mid-ninteenth century, steam-powered frigates were introduced, after which

The first Type-054A guided missile frigate, the *Xuzhou*

their displacements and weapons were gradually improved. In the early 1960s, the missile frigate made its debut. Afterward, it began to carry helicopters for antisubmarine work, reconnaissance, escort and other tasks.

In the PLAN's early days its largest warship was the frigate. Frigates were mainly of two origins: some had defected from the KMT Navy, and the others were KMT vessels captured in shipyards and ports. A representative frigate was the *Nanchang*. Its standard displacement was 1,200 tons and cruising speed was 14 knots. The main weapons were 120mm shipborne guns.

The most commonly used frigate in the PLAN in the early days was the Jie. After the end of World War II, to prevent the Japanese Navy from waging another war of aggression, the Plan either damaged or dismantled the large Japanese warships. The weapons and equipment on the rest of Japan's combat vessels were dismantled. They were distributed to China, the United States, the Soviet Union and Britain by drawing lots. The word "Jie" implied that the frigates were to be received or taken over. China received 34 Japanese warships, which arrived in Shanghai and Qingdao in four installments between July and September

6. THE PLAN'S MAIN WEAPONRY AND EQUIPMENT

1947. They were coded Jie 1 to Jie 34. The frigates in better condition were sent to shipyards for repair, after which they were equipped with weapons and called into service by the KMT. Other frigates were put in port for maintenance and other things. The PLAN took over Jie 5, Jie 12 and Jie 14, which were reconstructed as the frigates *Wuchang*, *Changsha* and *Xi'an*. The defected KMT frigates *Huang'an* (the former Jie 22) and *Hui'an* (the former Jie 4) were renamed *Shenyang* and *Ruijin*. The KMT frigate *Weihai* (the former Jie 6) was damaged and captured by the PLAN and renamed *Jinan*.

Other frigates were from different sources. The *Luo Yang* was the former Australian minesweeper *Bendigo*, displacing 880 tons. It was built during World War II and came into service in 1941. In 1946, it was sold to a Hong Kong company and renamed *Xiangxing*. Then, after being purchased by the People's Navy, it became a warship. The *Guangzhou*

Type-054 missile frigate, the *Wen Zhou*

was the former British Castle-class corvette *Bowmanville,* taken over by the Canadian Navy during World War II. It was launched in 1944. After World War II, it was purchased by the Investment Promotion Bureau to run as a liner between Shanghai and Tianjin. Because of damage caused by a typhoon, it was anchored in Shanghai and made into a warship in the spring of 1950. During the reconstruction it was fitted with 130mm guns and other Soviet equipment, and its combat capability was largely improved. This vessel participated in several sea battles near east Zhejiang Province. The frigate *Nanning* was the former Japanese Type-III coastal defense ship Coastal Defense 7. In November 1944, because the bow was damaged by U.S. torpedoes, the ship was towed to Guangzhou by the Japanese Navy. But the bow damage proved too severe to repair, so in 1955 the Jiang Nan Shipyard sent engineers and mechanics to build a new bow and weld it to the remnant latter part of the ship. The repaired frigate was renamed *Nanning*. This "half" frigate discarded by the Japanese was just like a withered tree coming to life again, and for quite some time it was the largest PLAN warship in the South China Sea.

The first-generation frigates cited above were the backbone of the PLAN's combat power in the early days. They performed brilliantly in operations to liberate near-shore islands and safeguard coastal areas and territorial seas.

In June 1957, the Type-01 frigate, built using Soviet technology, came into PLAN service. Its standard displacement was 1,249 tons, and the cruising speed was 14.5 knots. Its main weapons were 100mm guns, 37mm guns and several antisubmarine weapons.

In September 1966, the first China-made Type-65 frigates were delivered to the Navy and later put to use. The standard displacement was 1,263 tons and cruising speed was 16 knots. The main weapons were 100mm guns, 37mm guns and depth charge launching projectors.

In December 1975, China-made Type-053H missile frigates went into service. The standard displacement is 1,469 tons. The main weapons are 100-mm guns, 37mm guns, ship-to-ship missiles and depth charge launching projectors. Several improved versions have already appeared, and these ships can now carry helicopters.

6. THE PLAN'S MAIN WEAPONRY AND EQUIPMENT

The Type-054 missile frigates are China-made ships with a standard displacement of 3,696 tons and a cruising speed of 18 knots. The main weapons are 100mm guns, six-barrel 30mm guns, ship-to-ship missiles, ship-to-air missiles and depth charge launching projectors. This boat can carry one helicopter.

MINESWEEPERS: THE VANGUARD AT SEA

There are two kinds of mine warships: mine layers and mine countermeasure vessels. Dedicated mine layers aren't common, because aircraft, submarines and many surface warships can also lay mines. As mine countermeasure technology is demanding and challenging, special mine countermeasure vessels, including minesweepers, mine hunters and mine breakdown ships, have a significant presence in naval forces around the world. Mine warships are called "the Vanguard at Sea." They always perform the most dangerous mission of clearing the sea route. There is therefore an unwritten rule for navies everywhere: when meeting minesweepers, all warships and vessels shall pay tribute to the dare-to-die corps aboard. Even the main force battleship, which is much larger in size, salutes the minesweeper.

In the PLAN's early days, because it had no dedicated minesweepers, landing vessels and other warships had to be rebuilt to do the urgent task of minesweeping. In 1950, the KMT laid mines at the Yangtze River Estuary and sank and damaged many merchant ships in an attempt to paralyze the largest port in China, the port of Shanghai, and make it a "dead port." At such a moment critical to the survival of the economy of the newly founded PRC, the PLAN was ordered to sail the minesweepers refitted from landing vessels and to clear the sea lanes. Because they were able to ensure that the foreign trade at the port of Shanghai could continue unhindered, they contributed a lot to the economic development of the new China. Afterward, by introducing Russian minesweepers and using technology transferred for manufacturing, copying and improving, the PLAN finally had China-made minesweepers. These ships once helped the Vietnamese to sweep the mines laid by the U.S. Navy. They also took part in the Battle of the Paracel Islands.

Type-10 minesweepers were produced in 1956 using Type-254M minesweeper technology introduced from the Soviet Union. This ship's standard displacement is 628 tons, and the cruising speed is 10 knots. The main weapons are 37mm shipborne guns, 25mm shipborne guns, depth charge launching projectors and several sets of minesweeping devices.

The Type-081 is a medium-sized minesweeper made by China. Its standard displacement is 877 tons. The main weapons are 37mm guns and several sets of minesweeping devices.

MISSILE (ESCORT) BOAT: A SHARP SWORD IN COASTAL DEFENSE

The missile boat is a rising star in the PLAN. Production of this boat began in the late 1950s. It is a small-sized, high-speed surface vessel with ship-to-ship missiles as the main weapons. It's used mainly to attack large- and medium-sized surface warships in coastal areas. It can also do patrol, surveillance, antisubmarine and mine laying operations. The advantages of the missile boat are that it's small and high-speed, and it can maneuver easily and attack fiercely. But its endurance, self-defense capabilities and seagoing performance are fairly weak, which means it can't take part in long voyages and in fighting of long duration. It also can't go into battle in bad weather.

The earliest PLAN missile boats were the Type-21 and Type-24, which were manufactured using Soviet technology. Their displacement was only dozens of tons. Later, some domestically made missile boats also came into service.

The improved Type-037II missile escort boat was based on the Type-037 submarine chaser. Its standard displacement is 540 tons. The main weapons are 37mm shipborne guns, 30mm shipborne guns and ship-to-ship missiles. Such escort boats take in service in the PLA Hong Kong Garrison. These boats are named mainly after counties in China, for example, the *Fuqing*.

6. THE PLAN'S MAIN WEAPONRY AND EQUIPMENT

Type-022 guided-missile boats

The Type-022 guided-missile boat was successfully trial-produced in 2004. This is a high-speed, double-bodied stealth missile boat with a standard displacement of 250 tons. Its main weapons are six-barrel 30mm guns and ship-to-ship missiles, and it's fairly strong among small-size warships. Since its debut in the Qingdao Marine Parade in 2009, the missile boat has been attracting a lot of attention from naval forces around the world.

LANDING WARSHIP: THE AMPHIBIOUS WARRIOR

The landing warship is also called an amphibious warfare vessel. Its main job is transporting landing troops, weaponry, equipment, supplies, fighting vehicles and landing instruments. It can also provide fire support, command, communication and other assistance. The frequency and scale of landing operations during World War II were unprecedented, and in that context the rapid development of the landing warship was encouraged.

In the early days of the PLAN, the main combat landing force for liberating coastal islands was an array of U.S.-made landing warships from defecting and surrendered KMT fleets, along with some rebuilt

The PLAN's large landing ship, the *Kunlunshan*

civilian vessels. With the debut of the China-made landing warship, the old boats were decommissioned. Among the landing warships of the People's Navy, the large- and medium-sized ships are named after mountains in China, for example, the *Liupanshan*.

The standard displacement of the Type-072 landing warship is 2,800 tons. Its main weapons are 57mm guns and 25mm antiaircraft guns.

The standard displacement of the Type-074 landing warship is 536 tons. Its main weapons are 25mm antiaircraft guns and 14.5mm machine guns.

The Type-071 dock landing ship is the largest Chinese-made battleship. Its full-load displacement is about 22,000 tons. This type of ship can carry large-sized air cushion landing craft and helicopters. It can do ocean combat and other jobs. During the Qingdao Marine Parade in 2009, the first such landing vessel, the *Kun Lun*, carrying 260 marines, underwent inspection and attracted world media attention. In 2010, this landing vessel sailed into the Gulf of Aden for convoy missions. Its service in the Navy marks a significant enhancement of the ability of China's Navy to deliver amphibious warfare forces to central and far-off oceans. A second Type-071, the *Jing Gang Shan*, is in service. Its performance in all respects has been further improved.

6. THE PLAN'S MAIN WEAPONRY AND EQUIPMENT

SERVICE SHIPS: A GROWING FAMILY

In the service ship category are all the vessels that provide support for maritime combat, technology and logistics. They provide support and assistance for combat warships, undertake scientific expeditions, do oceanographic surveys, do weapons testing, do salvage-and-rescue operations, do construction, provide medical treatment, do personnel training, do vessel repairing and so on. Among these, the most common are the ships that transport and supply materials and personnel. The tonnages of the service ships in the naval forces of many countries are almost equivalent to that of the combat ships, and some are even greater.

During the 60-year history of the PLAN, the service ships have experienced great improvement and developmental momentum. In the beginning, almost all service ships were rebuilt civilian ships. Then, after several years' development, service ships of several thousand to even 11,000 tons gradually came into being. These ships provide necessary support and security for the People's oceangoing warships. The PLAN service ships can be categorized as support ships, transport ships, salvage-and-rescue ships, engineering ships, scientific research ships, navigation support ships, oceanographic survey ships, reconnaissance ships, medical treatment ships, repair ships, training ships and service craft. It is a growing family with more new members being added. Only a few Chinese service ships have names. Most have only a pennant number. Different from those of the battleships, however, the pennant numbers of service ships generally indicate the naval forces they belong to and their types. For instance, *Nan Yun XX* is a transport ship of the SSF. *Dong Jiu XX* is a rescue vessel of the SSF. *Bei Gong XX* is an engineering vessel of the NSF. *Hai Bing XX* is an icebreaker directly under the aegis of the Chinese Navy.

The comprehensive ocean depot ship has the largest displacement among Chinese warships and is an important type of support ship that makes it possible for the PLAN to sail the ocean. In the early days, the focus of the PLAN was coastal defense. So the warships' and vessels' scope of activities at the time was in close coastal waters. Comprehensive depot ships weren't needed to provide supplies. The ships fulfilling the supply task then were medium- and small-sized tank ships, water transport vessels and transport ships, mainly refitted civilian vessels. But in the 1970s, with the Navy's scope of activities expanding to the oceans, and needing to do support jobs for the test of the Navy's first long-range launch vehicle, four depot ships were built, each with a full displacement of 22,000 tons, and these included the *Taicang*. The cruising speed of this ship is 18 knots. It can carry over 6,500 tons of oil, 650 tons of water and over 165 tons of dry goods.

Afterward, two of these depot ships continued to serve in the Navy (now named the *Hongzehu* and the *Poyanghu*). One was transferred to Pakistan and the other was rebuilt as a civilian ship. In 1992, after the collapse of the Soviet Union, one tanker under construction was sold to China by Ukraine. The Dalian Shipyard refitted it as the *Nancang* (now the *Qinghaihu*). The full-load displacement of this ship is 40,800 tons, and it can carry 26,500 tons of goods and supplies. In 2004, two depot vessels with a full-load displacement of 25,000 tons each came into service. Their dead weight was larger than that of the first-generation depot ships. They were the *Qiandaohu* and the *Weishanhu*. Comprehensive depot ships have also been playing an important supporting role in many PLAN visits abroad, and they did convoy mission duty in the Gulf of Aden.

The light displacement of the hospital ship *Peace Ark* is over 13,000 tons, and its cruising speed is 18 knots. The body of this ship is white, in keeping with the convention of hospital ships everywhere. There is a distinct Red Cross symbol on the sides. On this ship there are operating rooms, testing laboratories, clean rooms, therapeutic rooms and other

Hospital ship *Peace Ark*

Experiment ship *Bi Sheng*

6. THE PLAN'S MAIN WEAPONRY AND EQUIPMENT

dedicated areas, as well as four lifeboats. This China-made hospital ship is the world's first specially constructed hospital ship of over 11,000 tons.

The oceangoing training ship *Zhenghe*, named for the famous Ming Dynasty navigator Zheng He, is the first special training ship made by China. It has a full-load displacement of 6,000 tons. Its main weapons are 57mm guns, 30mm guns and 65mm bazookas. There are navigation, communication and other training facilities on the ship. It can carry 250 trainees for ocean drills.

The first national defense mobilization ship of the PLAN, the *Shichang*, is a China-made ship with both wartime and peacetime applications. It is named for the modern Chinese naval hero, Deng Shichang, who died a noble death for his country. With a full displacement of over 10,000 tons, this ship can be used for navigation training, helicopter training, medical treatment training, container transport, national defense mobilization drilling and combined missions. For navigation training, the ship can carry over 200 trainees and 40 instructors at sea for more than 30 days. With the installation of a medical treatment module, the ship can hold over 100 doctors and nurses to do medical care training. The equipment and the standard of medical treatment on this ship are the equal of those of a city hospital.

The ocean training ship *Zhenghe* and the first national defense mobilization ship, *Shichang*, are both attached to Dalian Naval College, the only PLAN naval college with warships.

The Type-071 icebreaker is the first large-sized icebreaker designed and made by China. Its full-load displacement is over 3,520 tons. Its endurance is 13,000 nautical miles. The main weapons are dual-barrel

Comprehensive depot ship *Weishanhu*

Training ship *Zhenghe*

37mm guns. This type of icebreaker has done ice breaking and rescue work many times in the sea in north China.

The test ship, the *Bi Sheng*, is the China-made battleship for weapons testing. Bi Sheng was a famous scientist in the ancient Song Dynasty who invented movable type.

AIRCRAFT CARRIERS: FOR SCIENTIFIC RESEARCH, EXPERIMENT AND TRAINING

The aircraft carrier has the strongest combat capabilities in the modern world. It uses mainly carried aircraft to attack and defend. It embodies the science and technology, industrial development and defense capabilities of a nation. Aircraft carriers generally form battle groups with cruisers, destroyers, frigates, submarines and support ships to do various types of combat missions. In the modern world, the navies of the United States, Russia, France, the United Kingdom, India, Spain, Brazil, Italy and Thailand, among others, have aircraft carriers. The displacements of these carriers range from over 11,000 tons to 110,000 tons. The aircraft carrier can sail the ocean for long periods, and it is not only a keen weapon for combat, it can also do various kinds of non-war-related military operations.

It has been nearly a hundred years since the British Navy first refitted an old cruiser to carry seaplanes. The early fuels were coal and diesel oil. In modern times, there are a great number of nuclear-powered carriers. Early carrier aircraft were propeller-driven. Now, jets, helicopters, unmanned aerial vehicles, fighters, bombers, attackers, reconnaissance aircraft, early warning aircraft, antisubmarine patrol aircraft and other types of planes can be carrier aircraft.

On July 27, 2011, China's Defense Ministry declared, "China is now remodeling a worn-out aircraft carrier for scientific research, experiment and training." This aircraft carrier, formerly the *Varyag*, was sold to China by Ukraine. Work on it had stopped after the collapse of the Soviet Union. Since China's reconstruction work, the ship has successfully undergone several sea trials. The first trial of an aircraft carrier is a milestone in the development of the PLAN.

Table: Aircraft carriers in service around the world

Country	Name	Full-load displacement (tons)	Maximum Speed (knots)	Service Date
United States	Enterprise	98,770	33	11/1961
	Nimitz	100,850	30	5/1975
	Dwight D. Eisenhower	100,850	30	10/1977
	Carl Vinson	100,847	30	3/1982
	Theodore Roosevelt	106,250	30	10/1986
	Abraham Lincoln	112,440	30	11/1989
	George Washington	112,440	30	7/1992
	John C. Stennis	112,440	30	12/1995
	Harry S Truman	112,440	30	7/1998
	Ronald Reagan	112,440	30	7/2003
	George H.W. Bush	112,440	30	4/2008
Russia	Admiral Flota Sovetskogo Soyuza Kuznetsov	82,010	30	12/1990
United Kingdom	Invincible class *Illustrious*	22,710	28	6/1982
	Invincible class *Ark Royal*	22,710	28	11/1985
France	Charles de Gaulle	44,750	27	5/2001
Italy	Giuseppe Garibaldi	14,740	30	8/1987
	Cavour	29,870	28	2008
Spain	Principe de Asturias	18,950	26	5/1988
India	Viraat	31,640	28	1955
Brazil	São Paulo	36,130	32	7/1963
Thailand	Chakri Naruebet	12,660	26	8/1997

Submarines

Submarines can travel underwater and engage in underwater combat. Their main functions are attacking enemy surface vessels and other submarines, assaulting coastal targets, annihilating transport vessels and blockading sea lanes. They can also do surveillance, convoy work, mine laying, reconnaissance, transport, salvage-and-rescue tasks, and so forth. The advantages of a sub are its ability to conceal itself, strong viability and great endurance. A submarine can fight independently. At the same time, though, it's rather difficult for submarines to carry out underwater communication and target-observing tasks. Also, the living conditions on submarines are hard, the underwater sailing time for conventionally powered submarines is limited and subs expose themselves when they surface. On the other hand, nuclear-powered subs can do protracted underwater missions and carry nuclear missiles. This vessel is a military strength that is both concealable and maneuverable.

It was not until June 1954, when China took over the four Soviet submarines, that the PLAN started its own submarine unit. Presently, the Chinese Navy has nuclear-powered and conventional resource-powered submarines. The nuclear- powered subs were made by China, and most of the other type were also made in China, while a few are imports.

CONVENTIONALLY POWERED SUBMARINES: THE UNDERWATER RAIDERS

The conventionally powered submarine is a major component of the PLAN's submarine unit. There is the torpedo submarine (named for the Great Wall) and the missile submarine (named for the Long March).

The Type-033 submarine was manufactured at the Jiang Nan Shipyard using technology provided by the Soviet Union. It was delivered to the PLAN in 1965. This type of submarine is the one most commonly made for the Navy. Its submerged displacement is 1,881 tons and submerged speed is 13 knots. The main weapons are torpedoes and back-up torpedoes. It can carry mines.

The China-made Type-035 submarine was first delivered to the PLAN in 1974. Its submerged displacement is 2,325 tons and submerged speed is 18 knots. Its main weapons are torpedoes and back-up torpedoes. It too can carry mines.

The Type-039 submarine is the new generation of China-made sub-

6. THE PLAN'S MAIN WEAPONRY AND EQUIPMENT

marine. It has a submerged displacement of 3,461 tons and a submerged speed of 18 knots. The main weapons are torpedoes, back-up torpedoes and submarine-to-ship missiles. It can also carry mines.

The Type-636 submarine was introduced from Russia. It has a submerged displacement of 3,430 tons and submerged speed of 19 knots. Its main weapons are torpedoes. It can be fitted with back-up torpedoes and missiles.

NUCLEAR-POWERED SUBMARINES: A PRODUCT OF CHINESE DETERMINATION

In the 1950s, China was nuclear-blackmailed by the United States many times during the Korean War and Taiwan Strait crises. Chairman Mao Zedong once said, "In this world, if we don't want to be bullied, we can't do without this stuff (referring to nuclear weapons)."

In June 1958, Vice Premier Nie Rongzhen, in charge of national defense science and technology, presented a report to the CCCPC. He reported that nuclear-powered submarines would be the strategic weapons for future hegemony. He said that China must manufacture its own nuclear-powered submarines, to be able to counter threats by means of powerful deterrent strength. Mao Zedong and other leaders

The Type-039 conventionally powered attack submarine

soon approved the content of this report, and this marked the start of China's manufacture of nuclear-powered submarines.

The Soviet Union refused to support China in its determination to make its own nuclear-powered submarine. Chairman Mao famously said, "Even if it takes us 10,000 years, we must manufacture our own nuclear-powered submarines!" The resolute determination was self-evident. But at the time, China's chief designer for the sub, Peng Shilu, had only a toy model and two photos of foreign nuclear-powered submarines to learn from.

Later, when China's economic development was seeing tremendous difficulties, the manufacture of nuclear-powered submarines was suspended for quite a while. Still, a few continued to do theoretical research and experiments.

In 1965, the main work on nuclear-powered submarines was put back on the national agenda as the economy recovered. At this time, some suggested that due to the backwardness of the technology China should start by installing nuclear power in the external hull of a conventionally powered submarine. But this would take time, money and manpower. In the end, the decision makers decided to break with convention and adopt an advanced spindle shape for manufacturing, and this significantly sped up the R&D.

The first China-made nuclear-powered torpedo submarine, the Type-09I, came into service in 1974. It was named the *Long March I*. In 1983, the first nuclear-powered missile submarine, the Type-09II, was manufactured. In 1988, the underwater launching of a ballistic missile from a Chinese nuclear-powered submarine was a success. The PLAN nuclear-powered subs are named *Long March XXX*.

In 1964, after the successful detonation of China's first atomic bomb, the leaders pinpointed the two basic principles of a national nuclear strategy. First, never resort first to nuclear weapons. Second, attack vulnerable targets when making reprisals. The basic idea here is to use a limited amount of nuclear weapons to achieve an asymmetrical balance with formidable enemies that have many, so that purported enemies dare not use such weapons against China. And so China's nuclear policy is more for defense than offense.

6. THE PLAN'S MAIN WEAPONRY AND EQUIPMENT

To effectively pursue such a unique nuclear strategy, China must make sure that it's capable of inflicting a *second* blow. For this, the most effective means is via nuclear-powered submarine. Never being the first to use a nuclear weapon, if China encounters a nuclear attack most of its land-based strategic missiles and strategic bombers might be paralyzed. By contrast, the safer and more reliable nuclear-powered missile-bearing submarine would be the most effective main force for nuclear retaliation.

The dynamics and operating systems of the nuclear-powered sub depend mainly on nuclear reactors. Any slip-up will cause a nuclear accident and sometimes even trigger catastrophic disaster and widespread panic. Therefore, nuclear safety is always a big issue for all the countries with nuclear-powered submarines. Like them, China accords priority to this. China's first nuclear-powered submarine has been safely in the water for nearly 30 years. Among the countries with nuclear-powered submarines, China is the only nation that has had no nuclear-powered submarine accident.

So far, high-ranking military men from dozens of countries have visited China's nuclear-powered attack submarines, including "Father of the Nuclear Navy" Admiral Hyman George Rickover, the chiefs of the naval general staffs of the United Kingdom and France, and the commander in chief of Russia's navy, among others.

The nuclear-powered ballistic missile submarine *Long March 6*

On April 23, 2009, during the Multinational Naval Parade to commemorate the sixtieth anniversary of the PLAN, the nuclear-powered submarine *Long March 6*, the nuclear-powered submarine *Long March 3* (which holds the world record for longest sailing time underwater) and two conventionally powered submarines passed for review and inspection. This was the public debut of China's nuclear-powered submarine fleet.

Naval Aircraft

Before aircraft carriers came into service, the main equipment of the People's Naval Aviation was shore-based, fixed-wing combat aircraft, shipboard helicopters and a few seaplanes. In the early days of Naval Aviation, in use were various types of aircraft introduced from the Soviet Union. (Over time, these were replaced by China-made planes.) There were also some foreign planes in use. As R&D continues on Chinese aircraft carriers, the corresponding carrier-based fixed-wing combat aircraft will be developed.

FIGHTERS

Naval fighters are mainly for downing enemy airplanes, but they can also attack enemy vessels and coastal targets. They are the main naval force for gaining control of the air over water. Their advantages are high speed, good mobility and strong firepower. There are shore-based and carrier-based fighters. During World War I, Britain, France and Russia made fighters specifically for air combat. During World War II, naval fighters displayed even more remarkable combat capability. U.S. and Japanese fighters engaged in fierce large-scale combat many times over the Pacific.

Early on, naval fighter planes were propeller types equipped with machine guns or machine cannons. After World War II, jet-propelled naval fighters became the main force. Since the 1950s, fighters have been fitted with missiles and radar, which greatly enhances combat capability.

6. THE PLAN'S MAIN WEAPONRY AND EQUIPMENT

The fighters in service in the early days of Chinese naval aviation were the (Lavochkin) La-11 fighters, the (Mikoyan-Gurevich) MiG-15 fighters and other types introduced from the Soviet Union. Later, China made the J-5, J-6, J-7, J-8, J-10 and others.

The J-5, a high subsonic single-engine jet fighter, was a copy of the Soviet MiG-17. Its main weapons were the 37mm and 23mm aerial cannons.

The J-6 fighter was a copy based on the Soviet MiG-19. It made its first flight in 1963. It is a dual-engine supersonic fighter with 30mm aerial cannons as the main weapons. It can carry rockets, air-to-air missiles and bombs.

The J-5 and J-6 fighters have shot down or damaged many invading enemy aircraft—including the BR-57, the F-101, the P2V-7 and the F-4, as well as various other types of advanced aircraft—during air and sea defensive combat. They have been involved in significant military exploits.

The J-7 was a copy based on the technology of the Soviet MiG-21. The single-engine supersonic fighter made it first flight in 1966 and went into service the next year. Its main weapons are 30mm aerial cannons. It can carry rockets, air-to-air missiles and bombs.

The J-8 was a China-made dual-engine high-altitude and high-speed fighter. It made its first flight in 1969. Its main weapons are 30mm guns, and it can carry rockets, air-to-air missiles and bombs.

The new-type fighter jets of Chinese naval aviation force

The J-10 is a new China-made fighter. Its cruising speed is 590 mph, and its ceiling altitude is 59,000 feet. Its main weapon is the 23mm gun, and it can carry air-to-air missiles, rockets and bombs.

In addition to these fighters, the Russian SU-27 is also in service in China's naval aviation force.

BOMBERS

The naval bomber is used mainly for bombing enemy vessels, military ports and other targets, and for mine laying. Its advantages are great bomb capacity, long range and strong attack power. It can carry bombs, missiles, mines, aircraft rockets and more. In 1914, the British Navy equipped aircraft with bombs to attack German naval bases. Since then, the development of the naval bomber has been rapid.

This plane was in common used during the two world wars, then later in local wars. It evolved from propeller type to jet propelled-type. Its range and bomb capacity have also been greatly improved. All kinds of electronic instruments and radar enhance the combat capabilities still more.

China's naval bombers have developed gradually, from using the first Soviet bombers to copying them to improving on them.

The Ilyushin Il-28 was the Soviet first-generation light jet bomber. It had a maximum level speed of 560 mph. Its main weapons were 23mm aerial cannons and it could carry bombs or mines. In 1952, the Chinese Navy began using this type of bomber.

In 1967, China improved on the Ilyushin Il-28 and made the H-5 bomber based on it. This aircraft was soon mass-produced. Later, this bomber went into service in the Navy and in naval aviation. In the Navy, it generally served as a torpedo bomber.

The Tupolev-16 was a subsonic medium-sized Soviet bomber. It had a maximum speed of 616 mph. Its main weapons were 23mm aerial cannons. It could also carry air-to-surface missiles and bombs. In 1959, China adopted the manufacturing technology and assembled a complete aircraft. In 1966, China made its own H-6 by copying the Tupolev-16.

The H-6 would be the first of a series, as the aircraft would undergo many improvements. These improved versions would enter service one after another.

Presently, the PLAN bomber is the antiship bomber, H-6D. It can carry various types of antiship missiles.

FIGHTER-BOMBERS

The naval fighter-bomber is used mainly for attacking surface and coastal enemy targets from the air. The advantages of this aircraft are good performance in high and low altitudes, a large operating radius, great bomb load and strong penetration and viability. In the late 1940s, the United States equipped fighters with bombs, and these planes were the first fighter-bombers.

The major PLAN fighter-bomber is the China-made JH-7. This aircraft is nicknamed the Flying Leopard. Its cruising speed is 528 mph. Its main weapons are 23mm shipborne guns, but it can carry air-to-air missiles, air-to-ship missiles and bombs. In China's sixtieth National Day Parade, a formation of JH-7s flew over Tiananmen Square.

The Chinese Navy also employs the Soviet Sukhoi Su-30MK2. Its maximum speed is 1,305 mph, and its ceiling altitude is 56,800 feet. This aircraft has a flying range of 1,900 miles. It can carry various types of air-to-air, air-to-ground and air-to-ship missiles.

SEAPLANES

A seaplane is an aircraft that can take off, land and anchor on water. It is used mainly for reconnaissance, transport, antisubmarine operations and salvage and rescue. In the early days of the People's Navy, six Beriev B-6 seaplanes were introduced from the Soviet Union.

In 1986, the China-made SH-5 seaplane, based on foreign technology, came into PLAN service. Its maximum range is 2,860 miles. The main weapons are 3mm aerial cannons (Dorsal gun turret). It can carry

China-made JH-7 fighter-bombers, nicknamed the "Flying Leopard"

antiship missiles, torpedoes, bombs, depth charges and mines. It is used mainly in maritime reconnaissance, patrol and antisubmarine operations. It can also do surveillance and attack surface warships.

HELICOPTERS

The tasks that Navy helicopters can perform include antisubmarine operations, antiship operations, reconnaissance, patrol, minesweeping, warning, electronic countermeasures, transport and salvage-and-rescue. In 1942, for patrol purposes the German Navy began equipping warships with the *Bee Bird* helicopter. In 1944, the U.S. Navy began using helicopters in conjunction with submarine operations. Afterward, it became more common for navies to use helicopters. Modern shipboard helicopters can be mobilized for operations with warships in any waters. The main advantage of the helicopter is flexibility in takeoff and not needing a large landing surface. Helicopters can be carried on several thousand-ton light frigates and on 11,000-ton aircraft carriers.

Various types of helicopters are in use by China's navy, and the PLAN's antisubmarine operations, salvage, rescue, reconnaissance, transport and other combat capabilities are strengthened as a result.

In May 1980, China launched its first long-range rocket into the South Pacific area. Four shipborne helicopters, along with a task force, guarded the target area and salvaged the rocket's data compartment. The pilots

6. THE PLAN'S MAIN WEAPONRY AND EQUIPMENT

hovered above the falling point of the data compartment and divers jumped into the sea from the helicopters. They were able to salvage the compartment in only five minutes.

In the last 50 years, China's Navy helicopters have been through three stages of development: from shore-based to shipboard type, from a transport-centered to a combat-oriented application, and from coastal area to ocean-scope activity. The helicopter can assist in submarine operations, salvage, reconnaissance and transport, and it can guide attacks beyond the visual range.

The antisubmarine helicopter *Super Hornet* was introduced to China from France. The main weapons are antisubmarine torpedoes and depth charges. The Kamov KA-28 antisubmarine helicopter was introduced from Russia. The main weapons are antisubmarine torpedoes and depth charges.

The Z-8 medium-sized helicopter is equipped with sonar equipment, torpedoes and depth charges. It can work in submarine operations and do transport and other tasks.

The Z-9 helicopter is a light, multipurpose aircraft with 23mm aerial cannons as the main weapon. The naval Z-9 can be fitted with sonar, electronic reconnaissance and lifesaving equipment for work in submarine operations and for other tasks.

A shipboard helicopter

Marine Corps Weapons

The Marine Corps is an amphibious attack force with combined units. Its equipment and weapons are of various sorts and have different uses. Its functions encompass navigation, landing, airborne landing, underwater operations, land battles and antiaircraft defense, among other things. (The U.S. Marine Corps even has its own aviation unit.)

China's Marine Corps light weapons (including rifles, submachine guns, machine guns, mortars, flamethrowers, bazookas, and so forth) are similar to those of the Army. Among these weapons, the most characteristic is the amphibious warfare weapon. The main equipment of China's Marine Corps includes amphibious armored assault and fighting vehicles, amphibious tanks and self-propelled howitzers, among others.

The main weapon of the 63A amphibious tank is the 105mm gun. This is a key Marine Corps fighting element.

The main weapon on the Type-05 armored assault vehicle is the 105mm gun.

The Type-05 armored assault vehicle can carry more than 10 personnel. Its main weapons are 30mm guns and antitank missiles.

The 63A amphibious tank

Marine Corps equipment and weapons also include air-cushion landing craft, rushing boats, aerodynamic delta-wing airplanes, man-portable air defense missiles, demining equipment, chemical defense equipment, radiation protection equipment, diving outfits and other special weapons.

Coastal Defense Unit Weapons

In many countries, the approach to coastal defense has moved from a focus on coast-based guns to a focus on missiles. In the early days of the PLAN, due to a lack of warships and airplanes, the PLAN borrowed Army guns and deployed defense troops in certain coastal areas of military importance to guard against harassment and invasion from the sea and to defend coastal areas and islands.
In the early 1950s, longer-range coastal guns introduced from the Soviet Union gradually replaced the Army equipment.
In 1959, the PLAN introduced Soviet Type-542 shore-to-ship missiles. Then, after aid was cut off, China began to manufacture its own shore-to-ship missiles, with which the Naval Coastal Defense Units have since been equipped. Since the 1980s, all types of formerly fixed shore-to-ship missiles have been updated to be mobile, and the fuels in use are both liquid and solid. Presently, the naval Coastal Defense Units are all armed with missiles, and the PLAN's operating capability in coastal defense has been improved significantly.

The PLAN is equipped with 130mm coastal guns on a large scale. There are two kinds of guns: double- and single-barrel. Their firing rate is 10 to 15 bullets per minute. The maximum firing range is more than 15 miles. These guns can fire armor-piercing projectiles, bombs and illuminating projectiles.

The 100mm antiaircraft gun is a type in common use by the PLAN. It can fire air burst grenades and prefabricated fragment ammunition.

The shore-to-ship missiles in use by the Navy have progressed from being copies of the Shang You (SY-x) and Hai Ying (HY-x) series to the China-made Ying Ji (YJ).

The SY-1 missile was a copy of the Soviet Type-544 ship-to-ship missile. When its range could no longer meet the needs of coastal defense, the PLAN started making the longer-range HY-1 missile based on the SY-1. The flight speed and effective range of the HY-1 have improved a great deal since then. In 1971, mass production of this missile was realized. The weapon can effectively deter enemy forces within certain ranges.

The Ying Ji antiship missiles

The YJ-8 antiship missile is the China-made new type solid-fuel multipurpose missile. Its effective range is longer than that of its predecessor. This missile began to be produced in the late 1970s. It entered the naval force on warships and aircraft and in a range of coastal defense units.

CHAPTER 7

Doing Multiple Military Tasks

OVER ITS 60-year history the PLAN has always been an important part of China's fight against various security threats and a key element in accomplishing diverse military tasks. But the PLAN also does non-war-related jobs to maintain national security and protect lives and property.

Escort

FISHING PROTECTION AND ESCORT IN CHINESE TERRITORIAL WATERS

In the early days of the PRC, most of the islands along China's southeast coast were still occupied by the KMT Navy. China's warships and vessels were often harassed, and fisheries looted and burned by the KMT. Between 1950 and 1953 alone, KMT naval forces seized over 2,000 fishing boats and captured more than 10,000 fishermen.

And even since 1989, there have been more than 300 incidents of Mainland fishermen being driven out, arrested, looted and shot in traditional fishing waters in the Spratly Islands. Over 80 fishing boats have been captured without reason. More than 1,800 fishermen have been affected. Twenty-five fishermen are dead or missing. Seventeen others have been injured.

To ensure the security of offshore fishing, the People's Navy has been working to suppress bandits and protect fishing. The naval forces stationed in the Wanshan Archipelago, in Guangdong Province, have carried out this mission from the day in 1950 when they arrived in the islands. Early on, due to a lack of warships, the Navy had to organize armed groups to go to sea beside the fishing boats to protect them. In 1952 alone, 79 pirates were captured and eight boats seized.

In September 1952, Navy observation and communication personnel stationed on Nan'ao Island, including the famed sailor Qiu'an, were sent to the Nan Peng Lie Islands to assist the locals in organizing production and protecting the fishing there. They also formed mutual assistance groups and militia teams. In the early morning of September 20, more than 140 KMT solders, armed with U.S. weapons, invaded the Nan Peng Lie Islands on two warships and three gunboats. The PLAN soldiers and militiamen, including Qiu'an, fought back and defeated them—the KMT's three attempts to land on the island were in vain. Qiu'an fought to the last moment, until his ammunition was gone. Later, civilians built a monument to him on Nan'ao Island.

Gunboats protecting the fishing

7. DOING MULTIPLE MILITARY TASKS 135

From 1950 to 1953, the East China Military Area Navy dispatched 295 warships and other vessels 70 times, to combat the KMT Navy. They captured over 780 KMT personnel and sank, damaged or captured 85 vessels of various types. They also effectively protected over 28,700 fishing ships and defended lives and provided security for more than 350,000 fishermen.

The 1950s battles to protect fishing were fierce. One famous battle was at Maotouyang, in Zhejiang Province. The fishing grounds at Maotouyang covered 97 square miles, and as many as 5,000 fishing boats could come through from different parts of China. The fisheries were also on the southeast of Dong Ji Islet where the KMT Navy was stationed so protecting fishing in this area was rather difficult. To counter KMT Navy and Air Force harassment, the East China Military Area Navy dispatched frigates and gunboats to the south to assist the patrol boats in combat.

Between March 18 and April 28, 1954, the PLAN's *Xingguo* and *Yenan* fired on two KMT warships that had rushed at the fisheries, and they damaged the stern of a KMT *Yong* series minesweeper. The *Zhoushan* and the *Taizhou* patrol boat brigades also dispatched six vessels to fight the KMT *Yong* series warship and struck its deck. Four warships, including the *Guangzhou*, the *Kaifeng*, the *Ruijin* and the *Xingguo* engaged in artillery action with the KMT fleet. The leading KMT *Tai* series frigate was damaged. During ship-to-air combat, PLAN boats 612 and 505 were damaged, three soldiers died and five were wounded. China's Naval Aviation sent aircraft to the area and shot down two KMT planes. After this strike, the KMT no longer dared harass the fisheries.

After the 1960s, protecting fishing was still arduous. For example, the SSF alone had to dispatch 794 vessels and 262 aircraft between July 1980 and the end of 1982, for patrol, surveillance and other tasks, and was able to ensure the security of the fisheries as well as the Paracel Islands and the drilling platform in the Gulf of Tonkin.

In addition to the battle to protect fishing, the PLAN also helped the fishermen deal with the many difficulties and dangers that arose in their daily life. If fishing boats carried no fresh water, Navy seamen would provide it. If a fishing boat couldn't deal with the strong winds and large waves at sea, or if a fishing boat were adrift, the NAVY would tow it in.

Sometimes the fishermen couldn't accurately predict the weather at sea due to the backwardness of their communications equipment, so the Navy would inform them of the latest meteorological changes, particularly the typhoon trends. If a fishing boat met with a mishap, the Navy would try its best to salvage the boat and rescue the men.

Since the recovery and start of the growth of China's shipping industry, the PLAN has done more and more escort missions. Records show that from the early 1950s to 1964, alone, the PLAN dispatched more than 228,000 vessels to escort domestic and foreign commercial ships.

At the Military Museum in Beijing, a decommissioned warship is on display to commemorate an event that took place over 50 years ago.

On June 23, 1951, a PLA patrol fleet was ordered to escort three grain carriers and more than 900 fishing boats along the coast of Zhejiang Province. At the time, the vessels in this area were often attacked and harassed by pirates and KMT warships. The four patrol boats decided not to do the usual thing and accompany. Instead, they decided to ambush the pirates where they expected to find them. At daybreak, there was a heavy rain, and a thick mist hung over the sea. The sailors of the patrol fleet could only sense the enemy's presence by listening. Suddenly, they heard gunfire at Toumen Mountain Island in the southwest and set sail immediately at high speed. On the way, though, one patrol boat came upon a suspect situation and left the others to investigate. Two others

Boat 414, from the Battle of Toumen Mountain Island, on display at the Chinese Navy Museum in Qingdao

fell behind because of engine malfunction. Only boat #414 remained. It continued without hesitation in the direction of intense gunfire.

On arrival, the men on boat 414 found that a three-masted ship had intercepted the three grain carriers, and three other ships were approaching and about to loot them.

The men on boat 414 threw themselves into battle without delay. They fired fiercely at the pirates using their new 25mm bow guns, and they rescued the besieged grain carriers.

The pirate ships started to run, with Number 414 in relentless pursuit. When the pirates reached the sea near Toumen Mountain Island, they thought they could get help from the KMT. But the sailors on Number 414 pushed on. They rushed to about 330 feet from the pirates and began to fire. The stern of one ship received a direct hit, and the afterdeck was set afire. But then the water tank was hit and the water poured out and killed the fire. Still the men on Number 414 continued to fight, now at close quarters and with hand-held weapons.

At this critical juncture, the other three PLAN boats arrived to join in the fight. In the end, it was the PLAN that won the battle. One enemy warship was sunk and three others were damaged and fled. The pirates suffered more than 30 casualties.

The sublime heroism of the men of boat 414 in this escort mission became a favorite tale. And to honor its meritorious military service and heroic deeds, the East China Military Area Navy conferred on boat 414 the honorary title "Heroic Boat in the Battle of Toumen Mountain Island."

OCEAN CONVOYS

"This is the Chinese Navy escort fleet; if you need help, call us on channel 16." This notice echoes over the Gulf of Aden in both Chinese and English. For the Chinese and other vessels on the waters of the Gulf of Aden, this announcement has long since been a stranger.

"Mayday, Mayday!"

On June 6, 2011, the People's warship *Wenzhou* heard cries for help from the captain of the Pakistani cargo vessel *Hyderabad* over high-frequency radio. "A pirate ship discovered, 1.5 nautical miles, weapons and ladder being seen." At this point, the *Hyderabad* was 25 nautical miles from the PLAN formation. The *Wenzhou* now had a dilemma. If it went to rescue the *Hyderabad*, the six merchant ships it was escorting would go into the snake pit. If it didn't go, the *Hyderabad* would be in as precarious a situation as a pile of raw eggs.

The commander of the PLAN escort formation ordered its helicopters to take off and warn the pirates away. The *Wenzhou* would go to the *Hyderabad*, and he would dispatch ship-based vessels to escort the merchant ship group.

Twenty minutes later, the *Wenzhou*'s helicopters were flying above the *Hyderabad*, and the pirates had sailed away.

This was a tense episode for the Eighth Escort Formation of the Chinese Navy during what was supposed to be a noncombative escort mission.

In June 2008, due to the deteriorating security situation in the Gulf of Aden, the United Nations Security Council ratified Resolution No. 1816. Each member-state was empowered to "cooperate with the

On December 26, 2008, the First Escort Formation of the Chinese Navy set sail

7. DOING MULTIPLE MILITARY TASKS

Transitional Federal Government of Somalia (TFG) in the fight against piracy and armed robbery at sea off the coast of Somalia, for which advance notification [had] been provided by the TFG to the Secretary General."

The Chinese government decided to dispatch naval convoy formations to the area after getting the permission of the Transitional Federal Government of Somalia.

On December 26, 2008, three destroyers, the *Wuhan*, the *Haikou* and the *Weishanhu* support ship carrying two helicopters and dozens of special combat troops formed the first Navy Convoy Formation and sailed to the Gulf of Aden and Somalia for escort duty. This was the first time the Chinese PLA sent combat forces overseas to meet its obligation for international humanitarian operations. It was also the first time the Chinese Navy protected the security of ocean marine transport. The effort was an embodiment of China's self-image as a responsible large country actively fulfilling its international obligations.

In the three years up to the time of this writing, in the Gulf of Aden and Somalia waters, where sails and masts stand forest-like, the escort vessels of the Chinese Navy, Five-Starred Red Flag streaming in the wind, carry out China's promise to protect people and maintain security everywhere.

DRIVING OFF PIRATES WITHOUT FIRING A SHOT

On May 14, 2009, it was sunny. At sea, the water and sky merged into one color. The blue ocean was pure and clear. The warships here were sometimes accompanied by dolphins, which could have refreshed and gladdened hearts if the sailors could have taken a moment to savor the beauty. On this day, though, the warship *Shenzhen* and seven other vessels were moving in two columns, and the men on board were in no mood to appreciate the scene. They had to be on constant alert for unusual activity. For this was the Gulf of Aden, otherwise known as "the Sea of Horror" and "Pirate Paradise." The pirates rampant around here were a constant threat to the security of the passing merchant ships.

Escort formation helicopter hovering over escorted merchant ship

With the brisk sound of propellers, the helicopter unit, on alert all night long, now took off to patrol at the head of the formation. As the forward "eyes," the helicopters ensure that the escort formation can discover pirates early and make early decisions about what actions to take. The sailors call the unit "Squadron" over the Gulf of Aden. Sometimes, a helicopter crew has to tackle pirates single-handedly to drive them away.

"One mother ship towing three small boats sailing toward our formation from the left at high speed!"

And so it was that at 8:50 a.m. on May 14, this report came in.

After identifying the situation, the captain immediately ordered, "Helicopters, go closer and observe. Port Five, both engines four ahead. *Shenzhen*, go see. Report to the merchant formation and strengthen vigilance!"

The pirates are like wolf packs. When locked on a target, they flock together and rush toward it. So, as expected, the helicopters soon reported, "One mother ship identified 8.3 nautical miles to starboard. Eighteen boats sailing toward the formation at high speed."

Finding itself trapped in converging attacks, the People's escort formation faced a double threat. From the pictures sent back by the helicopters it was clear that the pirate mother ship was hidden in canvas. Meanwhile, nearly 20 speedboats were flying at full-speed toward the escort formation from all directions. There were up to five men in each speedboat. Great wakes formed as they drew near.

"Order! *Huangshan*, come immediately and escort the merchant ships. *Shenzhen*, sail out and drive the suspicious targets away," the captain ordered.

At this moment, however, the *Huangshan* was anchored nine nautical miles away, in standby mode. So it was left to the *Shenzhen* alone to respond to the crisis.

"In first-degree antipiracy deployment. Special operations troops and antipiracy emergency division, prepare to fight."

"*Shenzhen*, speed forward. Helicopters, circle close. Special operations soldiers, get ready on deck."

Receiving their orders, the men rushed to their positions on deck, while the warship moved at full speed toward the suspect small boats, while the helicopters flew low and hovered over them. For the pirates, this combination should have been a powerful deterrent.

At this point there was less than three nautical miles between the opponents. From the pictures sent back by the helicopters it was clear that the pirates in the speedboats were holding bazookas and rifles and from time to time aiming at the helicopters and warship.

"Prepare for battle!"

The special operations soldiers aimed their machine guns at the pirates as one man.

It was a split second that yet seemed as if time were standing still. The atmosphere was unbearably tense. The pirates obviously felt intimidated by the disposition of the People's combat forces. They didn't dare attack rashly. After a two-minute confrontation that seemed endless, the pirates turned and sailed off.

From discovering the enemy to driving them away, the entire process took 20 minutes. And during this confrontation, without firing a shot or releasing a bomb, China was able to establish its superiority over the pirates.

About to embark on a helicopter cruise

HERDING WOLVES

On March 18, 2010, Chinese merchant ship 9, the *Zhenhua*, didn't arrive on time at its destination east of the Bab-el-Mandab Strait because it was moving quite slowly. So as not to affect the sailing plans of other merchant ships, the Convoy Formation decided to dispatch the *Weishanhu* alone to escort boat 9.

At 9:45 a.m. on March 20, the heavy machine gunners on the *Zhenhua* were keeping a close watch on the port side.

"From *Zhenhua*, a suspicious target at 160 degrees to port!" the alert gunner reported to the command post on board.

The commander ordered the *Weishanhu* to sail to the port side of the *Zhenhua* to provide full protection.

In the blink of an eye, though, several groups of the spotted suspicious boats rushed in from all directions like hungry wolves chasing prey. These boats, of various shapes and sizes, kept gathering around and scattering. They approached the ship being escorted.

The eyes of the machine gunners were fixed on every move of the "wolf pack." They held tight to the heavy guns.

"Three nautical miles . . . two nautical miles . . . 1.5 nautical miles."

"Into first-degree antipiracy deployment!"

At 10:05 a.m., the *Weishanhu* signaled a fight. At the word of the commander, two red flares soared into the sky. Nevertheless, despite the warning, a group of the suspicious boats rushed toward the *Weishanhu*, to one nautical mile from the ship's port side.

"Fire explosive bombs and flash bombs!" the commander ordered.

Again, the small boats ignored the warnings.

At 10:39, several boats at the front came close to the port side of the *Weishanhu*. The commander ordered the sailors to fire warning shots.

The machine gunners modified their alignments and locked on the targets. Rattle, rattle, the sound of machine gunfire filled the air. A whitewater obstacle 10 feet high blocked the way of the boats. Suddenly, the air was still. The pirate boats stopped moving, drifted a while then took off in all directions.

The *Weishanhu* readjusted its course and resumed escort of the *Zhenhua*.

ENCOUNTERING PIRATES FACE-TO-FACE

"Approaching 200 yards from the pirate ships; the helicopters are totally within the pirates' attacking range . . ."

This was the first time Liu Jinkun, a deputy regimental commander of NSF Aviation, fought pirates head-on. It was also his strongest memory of his many missions to rescue Chinese and foreign merchant ships during three tours of escort duty. The following is from his memoirs:

> At 4:00 p.m. on August 6, 2009, the warning bells sounded. The Chinese merchant ship *Zhenhua* was being chased by suspected pirates in the west of the Gulf of Aden. This was the first time the PLAN Convoy Formation had entered the Gulf of Aden.
>
> The command post ordered us to take off immediately and rescue.
>
> One hour and 28 minutes later, the helicopters were over the

targets. I discovered that seven or eight suspicious boats, three to four nautical miles from the starboard side of the *Zhenhua*, were maneuvering to beset it at high speed.

"Bang, bang . . ." The special operations soldiers on the helicopters fired off two red warning flares in quick succession. There was no response. The suspicious boats were still maneuvering, attempting to find an opportunity to beset the *Zhenhua*.

At that time, I could see vaguely eight to nine people on each boat. The boats were all double-motored and sailing at high speed. Maybe they boasted a large number of men and didn't take escort helicopters seriously? They were still going their own way.

Our helicopters laid down anchor rods and lowered altitude to terrorize them with military force. Half a mile, a quarter of a mile, 200 yards . . . The pirates were just before our eyes. Meanwhile, we were within range of the pirates' weapons. The special operations soldiers had already opened safety locks and were aiming at the pirates, getting ready to pull the trigger. We could clearly see that the pirates' bazookas and rifles were targeting us. The

A crew on board paying tribute to the People's Navy

7. DOING MULTIPLE MILITARY TASKS

confrontation between two sides was intense. This was a life-and-death moment.

The helicopters hovered for a while. I dropped down without hesitation and flew over the pirates' heads, just above the surface of the sea. Violent water vapor surged on the surface. The lift forces of the helicopters forced the pirate boats to sway in the waves. Meanwhile, the explosive bombs fired by the special operations soldiers were exploding in the air, forming a strong deterring force.

After several minutes' confrontation, one of the suspicious boats bowed to the mounting pressure and turned to flee. Presently, the other boats turned away as well. To keep the pirates from coming back, the helicopters continued to hover over the merchant ship until the pirates had disappeared. Having made sure of the safety of the *Zhenhua*, we reversed our course and made a return trip.

REPELLING THREE GROUPS OF PIRATES IN ONE DAY

On the afternoon on August 28, 2010, the 6th Group Convoy Formation of the PLAN, escorting 21 ships of the 237th Group sailing east, successively repelled three groups of suspected pirate boats harassing the formation in the west waters of the Gulf of Aden.

At 2:50 p.m., the warship *Kunlunshan* discovered two boats, 4.5 nautical miles away and at the right front of the formation, sailing toward it at about 20 knots. The formation command immediately began Class II antipiracy deployment. The special operations soldiers rushed into position, and the helicopters lifted out of their hangars.

Meanwhile, the formation also discovered two boats speeding toward it four nautical miles to the right.

At this time, the formation command post made a strategic decision: "*Kunlunshan*, immediately go forward at full speed to intercept the boats on the right side ahead. *Kunlunshan* and *Lanzhou* to the left of the formation, immediately launch helicopters to drive the boats from your waters."

Several minutes later, the helicopters roared off the *Kunlunshan* and

A bird's-eye view from the escort formation of the Chinese Navy

into the sky. At this, the two boats to the right of the formation immediately halted. But the boats on the right side ahead of the formation kept coming. The formation command at once ordered the helicopters to fly to the right front of the boats and fire explosive warning bombs.

The *Kunlunshan* maneuvered at full speed to the right front of the convoy and was able to keep apart the interloping boats and the merchant ship formation, forcing the boats to turn and repelling them. Meanwhile, another helicopter moved to the back and fired explosive bombs to repel two boats attempting to anchor to the right back of the formation, until more than five nautical miles separated them.

At 4:16 p.m., all four boats took off, out of the alert range of the formation.

Only an hour later, though, danger again befell the formation. At 5:20 p.m., another orange boat appeared three nautical miles away on the right, ahead of the *Kunlunshan*. It was coming at the formation at high speed. The *Kunlunshan* immediately moved at the boat, and the ship-based helicopters again took off.

At 5:26, to deal with the approaching boats, the formation command ordered the special operations soldiers of the *Kunlunshan* to intercept and fire with heavy machine guns. After hearing these shots, four men on the suspicious boat immediately lay down. Their boat didn't slow, though. It kept moving toward the cargo ship the *Haijie* at the very front of the formation.

7. DOING MULTIPLE MILITARY TASKS

The helicopters with special operations soldiers aboard flew over the small boat. They hovered low and fired warning shots at the men in the boat. Finding no weakness to exploit, the boat turned and fled when it was less than one nautical mile from the formation.

During the three years the PLAN did escort missions, it dispatched over 8,400 officers and men and 10 groups of 25 warships and ordered 22 ship-based helicopter flights. By December 26, 2011, the PLAN had successfully escorted 409 groups of nearly 4,411 Chinese and foreign warships (some 47 percent were foreign). It had picked up and rescued 51 domestic and foreign vessels. It had aided four foreign vessels. It had been responsible for enviable military exploits, providing safety for both the escorted vessels and the convoy formation itself.

On February 23 and 24, 2012, the first International Symposium on Counter-Piracy and Escort Operations was hosted by the Navy at the PLA Naval Command College in Nanjing. Eighty-four representatives of international organizations, including the European Union, NATO and the Baltic and International Maritime Conference, and the representatives of 20 countries, including the United States, the United Kingdom, France and Germany, participated. At the conference, China's convoy operations over the prior three years in the waters of the Gulf of Aden and Somalia were praised, and representatives said they looked forward to cooperating more with China in escort work.

The representatives of the Chinese Navy suggested that the naval forces in each country as well as the international organizations should establish a mechanism for information exchange and should strengthen coordination, to push forward substantial cooperation in convoy escort work, to better serve the merchant ships around the world.

Captain Phil Haslam, of the European Union Naval Force (EUNAVFOR), told the press, "The naval forces around the

The warship *Xuzhou* rescuing the crew of the *Tai'ankou* by force

world have already fought shoulder-to-shoulder in these areas (in the Gulf of Aden and Somalia waters). Therefore, the cooperation and coordination among all parties on the operational and technical levels will be highly praiseworthy. The significance of such symposiums will drive all parties to reach strategic consensus at a higher level. We will clearly understand our mutual goal and the role we should play. Given such consensus and cooperation, we will usher in more efficient cooperation."

At the time of this writing, it is still not too safe in the Gulf of Aden and Somalia waters. Escort duty here is an arduous task, and the convoy officers and men of the Chinese Navy still have a long way to go.

On November 30, 2011, the spokesman for the Chinese Defense Ministry said that according to the relevant U.N. Security Council resolutions China will continue to dispatch naval convoy formations to the waters of the Gulf of Aden and Somalia for escort work and to further carry out international convoy cooperation, and that China will contribute more to safeguarding national interests and world peace.

"For the first time, China used military forces overseas to safeguard its national strategic interests, organized maritime combat forces overseas out of humanistic obligation, and protected the security of important transportation routes over ocean areas," PLAN commander Admiral Wu Shengli said.

During three years of convoy operations, the Chinese Navy dared to explore and innovate to enhance oceangoing operational capabilities, and it had many "firsts" in so doing:

- It was the first time the Chinese Navy organized warships, shipborne aircraft and special operations teams for joint transoceanic missions.
- It was the first time China defended national strategic interests effectively and displayed to the full the capabilities of the Navy in accomplishing multiple military missions.
- It was the first time the Chinese Navy did tasks for long periods at sea. In fact, the convoy formation set new records for continuous sailing time, for the most distant voyage and for flight sorties and flight hours by shipborne aircraft.

7. DOING MULTIPLE MILITARY TASKS

- It was the first time the Chinese Navy organized rear services and equipment support and accumulated an experience of synthesis support at sea.

These "firsts" embody the achievements of the PLAN during its 60-year history and show today's world its style and characteristics.

WITHDRAWING CHINESE CITIZENS FROM FOREIGN COUNTRIES

In the 1960s, large-scale anti-China rioting and violence broke out in a country in Southeast Asia. Many Chinese citizens were slaughtered there, and their property looted. The Chinese government ordered the People's Navy to do an emergency evacuation of the Chinese citizens there. To guarantee the security of the citizens and the vessels needed for the evacuation, the SSF of the PLAN dispatched 119 ships and 126 planes for the escort. The warship formation, with the *Nanjing*, as the flagship, did the job. This was the first time the PLAN evacuated Chinese citizens from a foreign country.

In February 2011, there occurred a social upheaval in the North African country of Libya. This may have happened on the other side of the earth, but it struck a nerve for millions of Chinese people. There were nearly 35,000 Chinese citizens living in Libya at the time. Their security in that country became the biggest concern of the people back home, as conflict in Libya escalated.

The *Xuzhou*, a PLAN ship on escort duty in Somali waters, received an urgent order and immediately set sail from the south of Bab Al-Mandab Strait to the Mediterranean. At about 10:00 a.m. on March 1, after five days' and nights' sailing, the *Xuzhou* rendezvoused with

In 2011, the warship *Xuzhou* sailed 1,000 miles to escort the ship evacuating the compatriots from Libya

the Greek liner *Venizelos*, which carried 2,142 Chinese being evacuated from Libya, and began to escort it. The helicopters on the *Xuzhou* took off to patrol and guard against any danger to the Greek ship. The special combat soldiers formed in battle array and stood ready for the unexpected. The *Xuzhou* escorted the liner until March 4, when they arrived at a safe area.

When the evacuated Chinese citizens saw the Chinese warships cleaving the waves and sailing beside them, a military operation taking place without the smoke of gunpowder, they were filled with a sense of pride and dignity.

International Humanitarian Rescue

THE LONG VOYAGE OF THE *PEACE ARK*

The Chinese hospital ship *Peace Ark* is the world's first hospital ship of 11,000 tons, designed and built by China. In wartime it can provide in its combat unit early and specialized treatment for the sick and wounded. In peacetime it can do maritime medical treatment training and provide medical service to officers and men in the warship formations and forces stationed on islands in remote areas. Various hardware facilities on the hospital ship are the equal of those of a Third-Class A-Level hospital.

Also, the *Peace Ark* reduces noise and dampens vibration when at sea. This ship might be called a peaceful modernized maritime mobile hospital. PLA officers and men at sea call it "the Ark of Life."

From August 31 to November 26, 2010,

The Chinese hospital ship *Peace Ark* sailing from the Kenyan Port of Mombasa to Tanzania

7. DOING MULTIPLE MILITARY TASKS

the *Peace Ark* was on a "Harmonious Mission-2010" to Asia and Africa, demonstrating the profound friendship between China and these regions. The ship traveled 17,800 nautical miles, for 88 days. The crew provided medical care to people in Djibouti, Kenya, Tanzania, the Seychelles and Bengal and to officers and men on the escort vessels in the Gulf of Aden. The crew provided medical checks for 1,417 people, saw 16,018 outpatients and treated 57. They did 95 surgeries and examined 13,425 more.

BRINGING LIGHT

Mr. Ibrahim was a 50-year-old pauper who had moved from Somalia to Djibouti. He had developed cataracts three years earlier, but because he had no money, the untreated degenerative disease cost him his sight.

But September 26, 2010, was to be a very important day in the life of Mr. Ibrahim. The eye doctors on the *Peace Ark*, from the department of ophthalmology of the Navy General Hospital, on that day gently removed the surgical gauze from Mr. Ibrahim's eyes. He could see. And the first thing he saw was the smiling face of the Chinese doctor. He grasped the doctor's hands and kissed them warmly.

Many similar scenes were played out everywhere. The Chinese doctors restored the sight of several Africans and were called "light bringers sent from God."

HER NAME IS CHINA

"Wa-wa-wa!"
Hearing a baby's cries, the Chinese surgeons at the naval hospital in Chittagong, southeast of Bangladesh, felt relief.

The woman in delivery, Janet, was a clerk in the local navy hospital. She was 36 weeks pregnant and needed a Caesarean section. But because she had a severe congenital heart disease, even the best local hospital couldn't help her. And if she were transferred to the hospital in the capital city of Dhaka, the trip could take seven to eight hours and she might not be able to bear the disruption of movement along the way. It was at this critical moment that she felt a glimmer of hope. The Chinese hospital ship *Peace Ark* had come to provide healthcare in her city. She was seen, and the associate chief physician, Chen Lei, in gynecology and obstetrics, decided to operate on her right away.

In less than five minutes, Janet's heart rate increased then sharply decreased. Her blood pressure also plunged, sending her into a state of shock. The mood in the operating room became somber and tense. The cardiology experts who were observing immediately took measures to alleviate her symptoms and lower her heart rate. Three minutes later, Janet's heart rate was normal. The loud cry of a newborn sounded. And a five-pound baby girl came into the world. Both she and the mother had come back from the gates of hell safe and sound.

The mother and baby were continuously tended for 48 hours. They had made it through the danger. Janet's husband, Anwar Hussein, who was in charge of logistics work for an institution Chittagong, Bangladesh, wept for joy. He excitedly told a reporter, "When I knew my wife's situation, I was scared to death. I was already prepared for the worst. I did not expect that the Chinese doctors could save my wife and my child."

To express his gratitude to the Chinese doctors, Hussein named his new daughter "Chin," which means "China" in his language.

LOVE FROM AN EASTERN ANGLE

The Chinese doctors and nurses on the *Peace Ark* are professionals in the remarkable art of healing. Among these, the chief head nurse of the Naval General Hospital and winner of the Florence Nightingale Medal, Wang Wenzhen, once led a medical team named for her on a round of visits in five countries in Asia and Africa. They not only provided medical care to the local people but also gave their love to them.

One hot afternoon, Wang Wenzhen and her team went to an orphanage in Kenya. The children were scared to see doctors and nurses with yellow skin. But one bold boy walked around Wang Wenzhen for a few

7. DOING MULTIPLE MILITARY TASKS

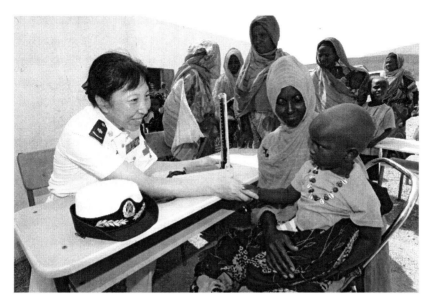

Nurse Wang Wenzhen with young patients

minutes, was gradually attracted by her motherly smile, and threw himself into her arms. He got a lollipop from Wang. At this, the other children all crowded around. Wang then took out a big cake, which to the children was just like doing magic. They jumped and cheered. They rubbed frosting on each other and called that day their Chinese birthday.

"Little Swallow, Little swallow, in bright clothes, it comes here every spring." I asked her, "Why do you come here?" She answered, "The spring here is the most beautiful . . ."

Wang Wenzhen taught this traditional Chinese children's song to the students in a primary school in the Seychelles when she visited there. The students sang and danced happily. The music teacher then asked the interpreters to translate the song into English and made a record of it.

In Bangladesh, a developmentally disabled child drew a picture of a tulip for Wang Wenzhen. Her mood was lifted when she looked at the cute picture: the beautiful tulips are a symbol of Florence Nightingale's spirit of humanitarianism, universal love and devotion.

Wang Wenzhen provided medical care and lectures on health at eight schools for deaf mutes, orphanages and welfare homes, winning her the appellation "Eastern Angel."

SALVAGE AND RESCUE: MERCHANT SHIPS IN DISTRESS

China's Navy has also rescued commercial ships and crews from many countries, including Britain, Norway, Germany, North Korea, Japan, Thailand, Yugoslavia, Panama, India and Indonesia. The work has strengthened the friendship between China and other countries.

On April 16, 1964, the British commercial ship *Crawford* sailed from Hong Kong for Dalian. When it was passing Dongfu Mountain in the Zhoushan Archipelago, it struck hidden reefs near the Sisters' Islands and was severely damaged—water was pouring into the cargo hold. China's ZhouShan Naval Base immediately sent out warships with rescue workers. They landed on the *Crawford* and made their way to the interior of the ship to drain the water and stop the leaking. The buoyancy of the ship was restored. With the help of the PLAN, the ship was able to go on. The Navy had dealt with the crisis and prevented a catastrophe. The British captain and his crew sang the praises of the Chinese Navy, their skill and their heroism.

In the early morning of December 13, 1967, a major fire broke out in the engine room of a Greek cargo ship anchored in Qingdao Port. The commander of the Chinese naval force stationed at the port organized a firefighting team of more than 300. Meanwhile, the ship's lighting

A Chinese naval ship en route to the North Korean port of Nampo at the Teadong River, to remove dangers to foreign vessels

7. DOING MULTIPLE MILITARY TASKS

circuits had blown, dark smoke was billowing in the engine room and flames were reaching higher and higher. The oil tank temperature spiked. The Greek crewmen told interpreters that the ship could explode within half-an-hour and that the Navy should evacuate immediately. But the officers and men kept working to put out the fire, with no consideration for their own safety. The captain of the Greek ship exclaimed, "I never saw such a brave force! They don't fear death!"

In the early morning of October 26, 1983, the U.S. drilling ship *Java Sea* was hit by a powerful typhoon during offshore work in the Sino-U.S. cooperation and development zone west of Yinggehai on Hainan Island. The *Java Sea* went missing, and this caused worldwide concern. The PLAN immediately dispatched 17 ships (including rescue vessels, frigates, submarine chasers and tugboats) to the area where the ship had lost contact. Divers went down more than 260 feet, to the bottom of the sea, for several days and nights. Finally, on November 3, they found the sunken *Java Sea*.

In February 1986, three cargo vessels from the Tian Jin Branch of China Ocean Shipping Company were trapped in five-foot-thick ice at the North Korean port of Nampo in the Teadong River. With the approval of the North Korean government, the China Ocean Shipping Company asked the PLAN to dispatch icebreakers to rescue the vessels. The Chinese Navy's ship C723 was dispatched to the port, and the officers and men worked hard to pull the three cargo ships from the iced-over area.

The PLAN has also rescued the commercial ships and crews of many countries, including Britain, Norway, Germany, North Korea, Japan, Thailand, Yugoslavia, Panama, India, Indonesia and others. China's 21st Escort Boats Team alone rescued 30 sick and wounded from 14 nations and regions between November 1969 and 1985.

Disaster Relief in China

China is one of the countries most affected by natural disasters. So the armed forces in China, including the PLAN, usually do the humanitarian relief and aid work there. Especially when dealing with the disasters that occur on lakes, rivers and seas, the Navy acts from a strong sense of duty. It has the special equipment it needs to do the job, and the skill to do it well.

Since the founding of the PLAN, this branch of the service has always had on its agenda the emergency and disaster relief mission and the protection of the people and their property. When a fishing ship, a commercial ship, a liner strikes a reef, is stranded, or is destroyed; when natural disasters (including drought, flood, earthquake and fire) imperil the people, the officers and men of the PLAN are on the scene to help.

Navigating through the dangerous channel

In 1953, natural disasters swept across Shandong Province, Henan Province, the northern parts of Anhui Province and the northern parts of Jiangsu Province. Getting food to the thousands of civilians in these areas was a huge problem. (Food was to be transported from Sichuan Province, but the ships to do this weren't equal to the task.) And so the 5th Fleet of the East China Military Area Navy and other units dispatched 11 vessels and 15 support ships from May to September, to buy and transport food and materials from Sichuan to the middle and lower reaches of the Yangtze River. The course of this voyage was dangerous. There are cliffs on both sides of the Yangtze between Chongqing and Yichang. The meandering river is rather narrow. And there are many reefs hidden in the rapid-flowing river. So it's very risky for ships to navigate this course, since they're likely to strike a reef and sink. It's even harder for medium-and large-sized vessels to make it through.

7. DOING MULTIPLE MILITARY TASKS

Still, the officers and men of the PLAN overcame all kinds of difficulties with determination and outstanding skills.

In 1956, the ESF dispatched vessels to Sichuan to carry out another food transport task. They moved 258,791 tons of food and materials, and this greatly helped the people in the afflicted areas.

SALVAGE AND RESCUE: FISHING BOATS AND SCIENTISTS

The PLAN plays an even more important role in rescuing ships and crews in distress. When there are strong winds, typhoons and/or cold seas, the Navy dispatches observation and communication units to assist the relevant agencies in communicating meteorological data, and it calls the ships engaged in offshore production back to shore to keep them safe. It also dispatches vessels and aircraft for salvage and rescue.

In April 1959, more than 2,000 fishing boats were hit by a storm in the Lv Si sea area along the northern coast of Jiangsu Province. The People's Navy dispatched 48 vessels and six aircraft, which rescued 31 fishing boats in distress and more than 190 fishermen.

In April 1960, a severe storm struck the four major sea areas of China. More than 800 fishing boats and over 4,000 working fishermen couldn't return safely to port. The Navy sent 58 vessels and six aircraft to bring back more than 260 boats. More than 530 fishermen in danger were rescued.

In December 1961, some ships from Liaoning Province sailed to the Zhoushan fishing grounds. Eleven got lost because they were unfamiliar with the route and they were sailing in strong winds. The Navy searched for 18 days and nights and finally retrieved them.

A 925 salvage-and-rescue vessel

In late February 1966, there was an unprecedented harsh cold-wave storm in the Yellow River Estuary and the river froze. The icebreakers sent out by the Navy worked four days and nights to tug all 300 trapped fishing boats out of danger.

And in January 2014, a Chinese helicopter from the icebreaker *Xuĕ Lóng* (snow dragon) spent seven hours lifting 52 passengers from an icebound Russian research ship, the *MV Akademik Shokalskiy*, to safety aboard the Australian icebreaker *Aurora Australis*. The captain of the twin-rotor helicopter, Jia Shuliang, told Xinhua News Agency he wasn't sure the ice would withstand the weight of his aircraft, but there was nowhere else to put down. Robert Darvill, chief mate on the Australian boat, told CNN news that the 52 new passengers on board were very happy to be there, and he thanked the captain of the Chinese icebreaker: "Thank you very much for your cooperation. Your crew has done the lion's share of the work and made Australia and much of the world proud." And so, after 10 days stranded in Antarctic ice, 52 scientists and tourists were safe, happy and on their way home.

FIGHTING YANGTZE FLOODING

In the summer of 1998, a catastrophic flood hit the Yangtze River. The PLAN ordered 2,600 Marine Corps officers and men to fly from Zhanjiang to Wuhan (where they transferred to buses) to participate in the battle against the flood.

On August 11, the Navy Engineering Academy's Diving and Rescue Brigade was sent in to deal with dangers in Hong Hu. The men worked day and night. They explored dangerous constructions and the affected areas of the 84-mile Jing Jiang levee in Hong Hu and Jian Li. Over more than 60 days of emergency and disaster relief work, the Diving and Rescue Brigade did more than 50 missions. There were 932 soldiers and workers diving; they worked for 414 hours and dealt with 93 areas prone to flooding. Because of their work, financial losses, that could have reached hundreds of millions of renminbi, were avoided. In October 1998, the Central Committee of the PLA conferred on this

7. DOING MULTIPLE MILITARY TASKS

The Marine Corps battling the flooding in *Wuhan*

group the honorary title, Heroic Diving Team in Combating the Flood and in Disaster Relief.

On August 20, an emergency was declared at the main levee of the Yangtze River in Jiayu County, Hubei Province. The men of the Marine Brigade received orders to deal with this sixth, and the largest, Yangtze River flood that year. Jiayu County is located on the south bank, in the middle reaches of the Yangtze. The county borders Wuhan to the north and is close to Dongting Lake to the south. To the east are the Jing Guang Railway and national road 107. The Marine Corps reinforced the main dikes to retain the floodwater, and by the afternoon of August 22 the water was under control and the levee protected.

Chibi City in Hubei Province is a famous ancient battlefield. There are 14 water gates on the main dikes of the Yangtze River, which is 17 miles away. Due to years of disrepair and being submerged in high water, the gates and culvert here couldn't withstand the flood, and there were leaks in many places. The lives of 130,000 people and the safety of 120,000 acres of fertile farmland were endangered. On August 24, the local government asked for Navy divers from to help mitigate the risk. On the morning on August 25, four PLAN divers came to the city and investigated the water gates. Along the bottom of these gates was a culvert that ran through the embankment, and the outer side of the gates was closed down. There were iron bars and a lot of rubble in the culvert. If something unexpected occurred (for example, the failure of a diving apparatus or exhaustion of an oxygen tank) when the divers worked in the culvert, they wouldn't come back alive. Yet, regardless of the threat to their safety, the divers managed to investigate three culverts and discover two leaks. This proved to be most important first-hand information, so the local Flood Control Headquarters could propose an action plan to rescue people and fight the flood.

After this, 48 amphibious reconnaissance team members dove into the water over an 11-hour period. They explored 12 water gates and as much as three miles of culvert. They discovered 68 places in need of repair. Dangerous situations were resolved in 16 places. And so they contributed much to fortifying the water gates and flood resistance.

WENCHUAN EARTHQUAKE RELIEF

The 2008 Sichuan earthquake was deadly. It measured a terrible 8.0 on the Richter Scale. The quake occurred at 2:28:01 p.m. on Monday, May 12, 2008, in Sichuan Province's Wenchuan County. The people in the affected areas suffered great losses. Soon after the earthquake, the PLAN dispatched 2,750 officers and men who marched more than 1,200 miles to the disaster area to do rescue and relief work. The Navy also sent three medical teams and two epidemic prevention teams to the disaster area and in so doing saved many from certain death.

THE PACES OF "BALLET GIRL"

On September 6, the opening ceremony of the Beijing Paralympic Games in 2008 was held in Beijing National Stadium, the "Bird's Nest." The disabled girl sitting there in a wheelchair drew the attention of the world.

7. DOING MULTIPLE MILITARY TASKS

She was sitting in her wheelchair in a pink ballet dress. When the spotlight fell on her, she slowly opened her arms. There was a flicker of hope and excitement in her clear black eyes. She used her fingers as toes to dance gracefully to Ravel's insistent *Bolero*. Then "Ballet Prince" Lv Meng lifted her high and spun her around and around. The audience could see her flowing and elegant dress and a look of sunshine and happiness on her face. When the "Ballet Prince" lifted her from the wheelchair over his shoulder, she straightened her right foot, and people saw one lonely red ballet slipper "standing" in the air and were moved by the girl's courage. Her name was Li Yue, she was only 10 years old, and she came from the earthquake-hit area of Wenchuan.

After the earthquake struck, Li Yue, in grade four at the Qu Shan Primary School in Beishan County, was buried for 66 hours. Her left leg was pinned by a cement slab; she couldn't move; necrosis set in. Rescue workers tried everything they could think of to extricate her, but they failed. As the seconds passed, everybody got more and more worried. At that point, aftershocks were still happening, and the building was in danger of imminent collapse. A doctor from the Navy medical team risked his life to amputate by the weak light of a flashlight in the narrow space where she was trapped, and Li Yue was saved. Under the care of the doctors and nurses she recovered quickly. Afterward, when she performed a program called '"Never Ending Dance" at the opening ceremony of the Beijing Paralympic Games in 2008, all of China was proud of her, and the world was deeply moved.

Li Yue in the opening ceremony of the Beijing Paralympic Games in 2008

On the evening of January 1, 2009, Ballet Girl Li Yue was excited. She had been invited to dinner with two people she loved the most and to whom she felt most grateful. Wearing a beautiful dress and sitting in her wheelchair, she came to the restaurant with her mother. As they entered, they saw the director of orthopedics of the PLAN General Hospital. Li Yue called sweetly, "Uncle!" Her mother explained that Li Yue chose such an intimate form of address because she felt that the doctors and nurses who rescued her in Wenchuan were all uncles and aunts and beloved family.

REMOTE-SENSING AIRCRAFT

China's leaders, including President Hu Jintao and Premier Wen Jiabao, also went to the hardest-hit areas in Wenchuan early on to personally direct disaster relief efforts, frequently gathering Party, government and military leaders there to discuss disaster relief plans over maps of the area. The clear and precise maps were witness to a great effort by the men of PLAN Aviation.

After receiving emergency orders for telemetry, the Cartographic and Geodetic Squadron, known as the "scientific research team," dispatched 22 Cessna Citation II helicopters to the disaster area. They flew for 115 hours in harsh weather. The area for telemetry and photography was over 323,000 square feet. The helicopters were able to collect complete and accurate post-earthquake terrain and landform information and materials, which meant the government could make appropriate scientific decisions about the needed rescue and relief work.

National Defense Scientific Research

With its continuous progress in cutting-edge scientific research for national defense and marine routes, China has increasingly enhanced its relations with friendly countries. Also, the state has ordered the Chinese Navy to perform huge missions. In executing these missions, the Navy's combat capabilities have been tested in a comprehensive way, which demonstrates as well the continuous improvement and modernization of the PLAN.

THE FIRST TRIP TO THE SOUTH PACIFIC FOR A CARRIER ROCKET TEST

May 18, 1980, was a memorable day. Many escort ships were deployed in battle formation. Red flags on board fluttered in the wind. Radar antennae were in motion. Excited voices were heard in rapid succession: "Signals received by remote measurement!" "Target discovered by radar!" "Target tracking going smoothly!" That day, China had a successful test flight of a long-range carrier rocket from its own territory to an ocean area of 70 nautical miles' radius, 4,350 miles northwest of the Fiji Islands in the South Pacific. The long-range carrier rocket crossed through the Southern and Northern hemispheres and splashed down as hoped. While the test was going on, a PLAN convoy formation safeguarded the flight and the landing. Then the vessels and warships, in formation, crossed the Equator and returned to the Northern Hemisphere. They arrived at Shanghai Port on June 1 and 2. The Task Force of the Convoy Formation had been at sea for 35 days, and the round-trip voyage was 23 days and nights. The total trip was 8,733 nautical miles.

Generally speaking, a long-range carrier rocket can fly more than 5,000 miles. So, due to the limitations posed by land, all full test flights have to be conducted over the open sea. For this, many measuring stations and large-scale measuring systems are indispensable,

The Chinese Navy Task Fleet sailing to the Pacific

and well-equipped measuring ships are needed in the sea where the rockets land. Also, during such a test, there have to be enough ships to do convoy, surveillance and support tasks. And after a rocket lands, it is imperative to salvage and retrieve the various recorded data of the flight. To accomplish all this, the People's Navy had to deal with many challenges to its test flight of a long-distance carrier rocket to the South Pacific.

For the PLAN at that time, the South Pacific was distant, and travel there unfamiliar. The Navy had to sail across four time zones, pass through four wind zones and typhoon generation zones, travel round-trip over 8,000 nautical miles and sail without docking, all of which posed many new challenges for navigation, meteorological observation, communication, logistical support and other work. There were 18 vessels involved—warships, measuring ships and support ships, whose total tonnage was 191,800 tons. The personnel involved came from eight fields and over 400 cooperative organizations. The high-tech instruments and equipment on the vessels were complex. For example, one measuring ship was equipped with 1,137 types of equipment and precision instruments. During the mission, the PLAN did many big things for the first time. For example, this was the first time using a first-generation, large, comprehensive depot ship to perform supply tasks in the Pacific. It was also the first time helicopters were mobilized for salvage work.

A shipborne helicopter flying to a salvage area

7. DOING MULTIPLE MILITARY TASKS 165

On April 28 and May 1, 18 warships set out for the Pacific in three waves. On May 3, when the Task Force had just passed the First Island Chain, the weather report team on the command ship discovered that a tropical depression cyclone had appeared in the northeast. On May 5, the cyclone started moving. It had two possible trends: gradually disappearing, or forming into a typhoon. To protect the precision instruments, commander Liu Daosheng ordered, "Turn south! Get away from it!" On May 7, the cyclone became a hurricane. Fortunately, by then the formation was already far away.

To keep communications open, the instruments were operated day and night. Over more than 30 days, there were nearly 5,400 communications via short-wave radio. The communication rate reached 98.2 percent.

In the month of May, the temperature can rise as high as 34 degrees Celsius near the Equator in the Pacific, and on deck it can be as much as 39.5 degrees. On the narrower destroyers, the conditions were even worse. The engineers in the engine rooms were working hard despite the heat. In these conditions, the water dispensers, refrigerators and air conditioners played a crucial role. On each vessel there were several medical personnel. The drinking water, food and personal hygiene were strictly managed.

Since the Xinhua News Agency had announced that China was to conduct a carrier rocket flight test, some countries had dispatched aircraft and ships to track and spy on the PLAN task force. They showed great interest in the China-made first-generation comprehensive depot ships and the replenishment devices alongside. (These did ship-side replenishment for the destroyers, which in general plays a significant role in enhancing the viability and combat capabilities of warships and other vessels.) Almost every time the X615 and X950 did a replenishment, foreign aircraft and ships took pictures and/or observed nearby. U.S. Navy reconnaissance aircraft even hovered high in the sky for an hour and a half. The New Zealand research vessel *Monowai* sent a signal: "We are very interested in your exercise. Please allow us to sail and observe on your starboard side." Overall, the convoy had to deal with some complicated circumstances, according to commands and in accord with foreign policy. Some captains from foreign vessels were invited to board the Chinese warships to observe.

On May 18, the first long-range carrier rocket manufactured by China was launched from the Jiuquan Satellite Launch Center (JSLC). In the course of 30 minutes it went from the Southern to the Northern Hemisphere and had a pinpoint landing. At 10:30 a.m., the data compartment hit the ocean and the surrounding water turned green from colorants. Chinese destroyers and workboats immediately arrived to protect the compartment. When it had discovered the rocket at 6,600 feet, airborne survey helicopter 179 had taken pictures as the rocket fell and identified the splashdown position of the data compartment. Shortly after, under the guidance of that helicopter, helicopter 172 raced in the rain to hover above the position. It took only five minutes and 20 seconds for divers to salvage the data compartment.

Shortly after this, the military officer at the U.S. Embassy in China made an appointment to meet the persons in charge of the Chinese Navy forces stationed in Shanghai. He took out U.S. reconnaissance aircraft photos of the People's Navy doing replenishments in the Pacific and said, "You have solved the problem of replenishment. The Chinese Navy is now welcome to visit our country!"

ESTABLISHING THE GREAT WALL STATION IN ANTARCTIC

Between November 20, 1984, and April 10, 1985, China sent fleets of ships to Antarctica for the first time to establish China's first scientific research base there, namely, the Great Wall Station. This was also the first time the Chinese Navy reached Antarctica.

Antarctica is the only continent in the world with no aborigines or plants. It lies in deep slumber at the southernmost point on Earth. There are rich mineral resources and marine life resources here. The area exerts great influence on the environments of the world's oceans. Over more than 200 years, navigators and scientists have been exploring this mysterious land, and many have lost their lives doing so. By the end

7. DOING MULTIPLE MILITARY TASKS

The inauguration ceremony for China's Great Wall Station

of 1984, 18 countries had established survey and observation stations in Antarctica.

In May 1983, with the ratification of the National People's Congress, China's Antarctic Investigation Committee was established. Various projects preparatory to scientific expeditions to the Antarctic were begun. In July 1984, with the ratifications of China's State Council and the Central Military Commission of the PRC, the National South Pole Investigation Commission took charge of comprehensive expeditions. This Antarctic Expedition Team is comprised of the ocean research ship *Xiangyanghong 10* from the National Bureau of Oceanography, and PLAN salvage and rescue ship J121. There were 308 involved in the tasks for the long voyage.

Ship J121 is a China-made ocean salvage and rescue ship. It entered service in 1982. The ship is 512 feet long and 68 feet wide. Its full-load displacement is 13,000 tons, and its endurance range is 18,000 nautical miles. It can withstand hurricanes. The PLAN assignments were to transport materials and equipment, to participate in the establishment of the scientific investigation station and to do maritime rescue and navigation training, among other things. It was decided that the

PLAN ship J121 on arrival on its first South Pole expedition

expedition warships and other vessels would also pay visits to the port of Ushuaia in Argentina and the port of Punta Arenas in Chile.

On November 22, 1984, the Scientific Formation of the People's Navy embarked on the long voyage to blaze a route from China to the Antarctic. This would be a long journey full of hardships and dangers. The round-trip voyage would exceed 22,900 nautical miles, which is greater than the circumference of the Earth.

Before setting sail, ship J121 consulted meteorological data and information and was able to accurately calculate the stabilities and wind resistance of its hull for the route selected by command. Static and dynamic curves of stability were even drawn. Deployment diagrams were provided for the weight- and center-of-gravity positions of the cumbersome equipment on board (including cars, forklift trucks, cranes, compressors, bulldozers, oil tanks and engines).

The Expedition Team passed the Miyako Strait in the Amami Archipelago, crossed the Pacific, and finally entered the Atlantic, heading for the Antarctic. The Team passed through two typhoon-generation zones, several rocky water areas and the roaring westerlies. It made it through the swells of the westerlies and made it through the dangerous Drake Passage, nicknamed the "Navigators' Tomb." During the voyage, the support for the right engine's water cooling tube broke and the sleeve fell off. The Team was able to deal with the mechanical failure. In the early morning of December 26, 1984, the ship entered Min Fang Bay on King George Island, Antarctica.

During the building of Great Wall Station, the Navy personnel were immersed in the icy water along with the Expedition Team members. It took them only five days to build an improvised discharging dock. On January 20, the construction brigade, comprised of Navy commandos and Expedition Team members, built the principal part of the project under unified command. The commandos brought their own expertise into full play: they took charge of designers, draftsmen, engravers, welders, woodworkers and ironworkers. The engineers responsible for dynamiting joined in, as well. The principal part of the station was built in 25 days, from groundbreaking to interior decoration. It took just 45 days to build the entire station.

The Expedition Team members were proud of the Navy personnel, saying, "The Navy has strong technical forces. There are all kinds of talents! These talents are not only for the military but for civil society, too!"

On February 21, 1985, when the people at home were celebrating the Spring Festival, more than 400 Chinese Expedition Team members and Navy personnel were holding an inauguration ceremony in front of the main orange building of the Great Wall Station on King George Island, celebrating the establishment of the first Chinese expedition station in Antarctica. A copper plaque in the center of the hall bears an inscription by Deng Xiaoping, "Devoted to the peaceful utilization of Antarctica." The president of the delegation, Wu Heng, read a congratulatory telegram from the State Council. The chiefs and deputy chiefs of the expedition stations of Chile, Argentina, Brazil, Poland, the Soviet Union and Uruguay were invited to attend the ceremony. Various kinds of meteorological, communication and computer instruments were installed in the newly completed Great Wall Station. A 10-foot-tall anchor was placed outside the station, inscribed "To commemorate the arrival of 308 officers and men of the Chinese PLAN in Antarctica."

ESTABLISHING AN OCEANOGRAPHY OBSERVATORY

In 1986, China proposed at the conference of the United Nations Commission on Oceanography that to carry out global joint measurement of the sea level it would be necessary to establish an observation station in the Spratly Islands. The proposal gained global support. The World Oceanic Organization adopted the proposal and named the station Station 74 in the global sea-level observation system.

On April 20, 1987, the 14th Conference of the Inter-Governmental Oceanographic Commission on Oceanography of the United Nations Educational, Scientific and Cultural Organization (UNESCO) was held in France. At the conference, a program for a global sea level observation network was put forward. China would be required to establish five observation stations, including one in the Spratly Islands and one in the Paracel Islands. The measurement data would be shared with other countries. The proposal provided that China would be the nation responsible for establishing the observation station in the Spratly Islands. It was also noted that the islands are under the control of the Chinese Government, as would be the station to come.

On May 15, a Chinese Expedition Team to the Spratly Islands comprising 44 professional and technical personnel set sail in the scientific survey ship *Xiangyanghong 5* to the waters near the Spratly Islands to look for the most suitable location for an observation station. The exploration took 23 days. The voyage totaled 2,153 nautical miles. The Team

China's Ocean Observation Station on Fiery Cross Reef

7. DOING MULTIPLE MILITARY TASKS

looked at potential sites from the points of view of topography, geology, hydrology, meteorology, chemistry and biology. They did a delicate survey of Fiery Cross Reef, in the southwest part of the Spratly Islands.

Fiery Cross Reef (9°35'N., 112°54'E.) is a long and elliptical-shaped reef 14.5 nautical miles long and four nautical miles wide. There is a lagoon at the center. There are almost 10 drying reef plates surrounding the atoll. The Reef is about 560 nautical miles from Yulin Naval Port, in Hainan Province. The reef plate runs from west to east. It lies at the intersection of the central route of the South China Sea (from Hong Kong to Singapore) and the Nanhua Bank of the Donghai Channel (a deep waterway of about 280 nautical miles running from east to west in the South China Sea).

Fiery Cross Reef has many advantages as an observation post, including convenient access to transportation, a vast sea area, a flat reef plate and a good geologic base. Also, there are reefs here in rows or sheets that have a wave-damping effect. The waters on the south of the reef plate are conducive to mooring and anchoring. Based on their analysis and investigation, the Expedition Team chose this area for the observation station.

In accord with the decisions of the China State Council and the Military Commission of the CCCPC, the PLAN built an ocean observation station on Fiery Cross Reef from February to August 1988 at the request of UNESCO. With the establishment of the Ocean Observation Station, China could make its own contribution to the work of sea-level measurement taking place around the world. This would have important implications for future marine scientific research and the harnessing of marine resources.

From February 1 to 7, 1988, 11 vessels—including ESF landing ship 929, SSF ship 833, south dredges 613 and 609, south barges 42 and 45, landing ship 8535, floating crane vessel *Dali*, semi-subdiving barge *Zhongren 1*, among others—arrived at Fiery Cross Reef loaded with the equipment to establish the station and the construction personnel on board. The Navy dispatched combatant ships and large-scale auxiliary ships to examine on the spot 11 islands and reefs, including Da Guan Island, Cuarteron Reef, East Reef, South Reef, Johnson South Reef,

Lansdowne Reef, South Reef and Subi Reef. It also sent out aircraft to beef up patrols around the Spratly Islands.

After half a year's work, on August 2, 1988, the first Ocean Station in the Spratly Islands, the Ocean Observation Station on Fiery Cross Reef, was finished. The observation station is a two-story building of over 10,800 square feet and it stands as an outpost in the South China Sea. China's flag flies atop the building. There are automatic observation systems inside, responsible for recording water levels, waves, water temperature, salinity, wind direction, wind speed, atmospheric pressure, temperature and other hydrological and meteorological data. Computer systems also process, save and print various meteorological data. Materials and data can then be sent to Mainland China and/or domestic and foreign meteorological organizations to ensure the safety of ships passing through the area.

While the PLAN was building the Ocean Observation Station on Fiery Cross Reef, it was also constructing some semi-permanent houses, on five reefs, that can withstand 12 Bft winds. These houses are high up on the Subi Reef, Johnson South Reef, Cuarteron Reef, Gaven Reef and Hughes Reef plates.

Houses high up on the reef plate of the Spratly Islands

7. DOING MULTIPLE MILITARY TASKS

Since the completion of the station, observation staff and Navy personnel work in regular shifts. They not only endure the heat and high temperatures but also once a typhoon. In November of the year the station was built, it was hit by a hurricane. Despite strong winds and tall waves, station work proceeded as usual. Accurate and reliable data and materials about the environmental conditions of the ocean were still collected, despite the harsh conditions. Since the station was built, PLAN personnel have meticulously observed and recorded wind direction, wind speed, tide levels, temperature and 20 other factors and provided accurate weather and oceanic forecasts. Over more than two decades so far, this observation station has provided more than 1.4 million sets of hydro-meteorological data to UNESCO and national meteorological departments and it has a record of zero defects in over 7,000 consecutive days. Such an achievement won high praise from UNESCO and the Chinese State Oceanic Administration.

TRACKING AND MEASURING COMMUNICATIONS SATELLITES

On April 8, 1984, China launched an experimental communications satellite and successfully positioned it at a designated point over the Equator, at E 125°. The equipment and instruments on the satellite functioned perfectly. Tests of communication, broadcast and television transmission all went well.

To be able to launch such a satellite, the PLAN needed to establish several tracking and measuring stations along a navigation route of over 3,700 miles, from the domestic launching site to orbit over the South Pacific. These stations were built on three oceangoing vessels fitted with various precision instruments. The vessels were responsible for trajectory and remote measuring during the maritime flight stages. Launching and measuring procedures are as precise as millisecond and microsecond measuring.

The SSF ship, J506, did the tracking and measuring. The J506 is a China-made ocean rescue ship with a displacement of 11,000 tons. It was incorporated temporarily into the Telemetry Ship Team to which the National Defense Scientific Industry Council belongs. Its pennant number was changed to *Yuanwang 3*. It sailed to the measuring points in the Pacific and did research and experiments. The ship sailed twice to the Pacific and did detailed research on conditions in the area. It also did combined adjustment of remote measuring and communication. The process took over 80 days.

After ensuring that all was well, the ship began direct preparations for the launch of the communications satellite.

On March 26, 1984, on orders from launch command, J506 sailed to the Pacific for a third time. At 2:00 a.m. on March 29, it was at standby position, on schedule. At 2:00 p.m. on April 8, the ship began a five-hour pre-launch preparation and sailed to the planned point on schedule. Satellite launch command asked for the measuring point at which J506 was to measure for five minutes data from the satellite as it flew over the ship. In fact, the ship was able to track the satellite for twice as long and so accomplished its mission.

CHAPTER 8

The Course of Friendship

THE GERMAN TOWN OF Wilhelmshaven has a small population of tens of thousands. One day in the late autumn of 2001, the sleepy town was awakened. Locals, students, Chinese citizens and others from abroad rushed to the navy base at the port. When they arrived there, they found four visiting Chinese warships on a tour of European countries. On this, the ships' first day in Wilhelmshaven, the people were free to visit them.

During their stay the Chinese were treated warmly by local governments, by other naval forces and by the people. The visit would be a rare opportunity to enhance mutual understanding between the visiting sailors and the locals.

China's navy is an international force whose exchanges and visits with the navies of other countries are frequent and ardent. Since the 1980s, the Chinese Navy has gradually opened up. The PLAN actively encourages high-level military exchanges and visits and port calls through visits by warships, maritime joint exercises and direct contact at the highest level of the world's navies. There are also bilateral military negotiations, multilateral navy forums, military academic exchanges, multinational military activities and many other communication channels and approaches. These are expected to largely enhance military and diplomatic communication between China and other nations, deepening understanding, trust and friendship between naval forces around the world.

China's Warships Abroad

Warships are mobile territory, and so visits abroad by warships and Navy vessels are always viewed as a most important part of military diplomacy. Such visits are also an embodiment of a nation's maritime strength. As part of its embracing and opening up to the world, the Chinese Navy is making voyages of friendship to every corner of the globe. Since visiting overseas for the first time in 1985, Chinese Navy formations have so far sailed to 50 countries in a spirit of peace and friendship. And now, in the new century, these visits are happening more often.

PLAN'S FIRST VISIT TO THE THREE COUNTRIES IN SOUTH ASIA

For a long time after its establishment in April 1949, the PLAN didn't send warships and other Navy vessels out of China. Even in 1965, when the Soviet Union's Pacific Fleet visited Shanghai and that nation invited China to pay a return visit, China was not able to reciprocate. Because of to the backwardness of its equipment, China's Navy didn't have warships capable of making such a long voyage and withstanding the strong

On November 29, 1985, Chinese warships entered the Indian Ocean for the first time

8. THE COURSE OF FRIENDSHIP

winds and waves they would surely encounter along the way. In fact, it would turn out that the PLAN wouldn't be able to visit the Soviet Union for another 30 years.

Finally, in 1985, the Chinese Navy dispatched the missile destroyer *He Fei* and the comprehensive depot ship *Fengcan* to Pakistan, Sri Lanka and Bangladesh. This was the first time a PLAN formation had gone to another country. On November 16, the Visiting Formation, under ESF commander Nie Kuiju, set sail from Wusong Naval Port in Shanghai. After several days' voyage, the ships sailed into the Indian Ocean, at 4:00 p.m. on the 29th. In accordance with navy tradition, the personnel on board held a memorial ceremony, and there was a military parade at sea to welcome the visitors from China.

The ships' first destination was Karachi, which has the largest port in Pakistan. This port is deep and wide enough for vessels of hundreds of thousands of tons, and it is also Pakistan's naval base. In the early morning of December 8, the Chinese Navy warships sailed to a point 20 nautical miles from Karachi and were met by two Pakistani submarine chasers coming to welcome them. Under escort by the Pakistan boats, the Chinese sailed into Karachi to the sound of a 21-gun salute, while colorful flags at the port danced in the wind. The commanders and officers from the Pakistani navy base were lined up, ready to greet their Chinese guests, and a military band was playing the national anthems of Pakistan and China. When the Chinese sailors reached land, Pakistani officers, sailors, women and children in traditional South Asian clothes held out flowers to greet them.

The acting chief of staff of the Pakistan Navy said, "Pakistan is the first country visited by the Chinese Navy. This is proof of the friendship between the two countries."

On the wall of a corridor at the marine training center in Pakistan, the Chinese visitors were surprised to discover this sign: "Want to learn new things? Go to China!" The commander of the training school responsible for receiving the Chinese said, "Our Chinese friends are warm-hearted and sincere. You have given us advanced equipment and instruments. We Pakistanis are grateful and very glad to see that China is becoming stronger day by day!"

On December 18, after their visit to Karachi, the Chinese ships arrived at the second stop in their voyage, Colombo, Sri Lanka. While the sailors were visiting the new parliament building there, the Prime Minister of Sri Lanka was in a meeting with his ministers. On learning of the arrival of their Chinese friends, they broke with protocol by adjourning to welcome their guests.

Nie Kuiju reviewing an honor guard during the grand welcoming ceremony

The Sri Lankan escorts said, "The Chinese people have always selflessly helped and supported us. This Bandaranaike Memorial International Conference Hall and the lagerstroemia trees planted by Premier Zhou Enlai in the Tropical Botanical Garden of Kandy will always be a reminder to the Sri Lankans of their friendship with the Chinese."

The Permanent Secretary of the Defense Ministry of Sri Lanka said, "In the fifteenth century, the Chinese navigator Zheng He sailed to Sri Lanka, and this marked the beginning of the friendship between our two countries." Asoka de Silva, the commander of the Sri Lankan naval force said, "The Chinese Navy has begun to visit other countries 36 years after it was founded. We have waited too long for this moment! We hope you'll come year after year."

By December 30, after the ships visited Bangladesh, the PLAN visit was completed. But on their way back to China, something interesting happened. Before the ships had set out on their South Asian voyage, the Chinese Navy and the U.S. Navy had reached an agreement dealing with landing and mutual visits. The U.S. Pacific Fleet dispatched three warships to wait for the Chinese ships in the South China Sea. Several days later, the Chinese rendezvoused with the U.S. warships. The two sides raised signal flags, and the officers and men lined up to salute each other. The plan was then that the two nations would send personnel to

8. THE COURSE OF FRIENDSHIP

visit on each other's vessels. But there were strong winds and large waves at the time, and the Chinese suggested that this plan be aborted. Nevertheless, for over an hour the United States attempted unsuccessfully to put down landing boats. Overall, the meeting between the Chinese and the U.S. warship formations was friendly and was concluded amicably.

A SINGLE SHIP CROSSES THE PACIFIC

On the morning of April 12, 1989, it was a pleasant day in Hawaii. The breeze was gentle and the sun was warm. But the bucolic scene was rudely interrupted by the sound of a siren. The Chinese naval training ship *Zhenghe* was moving slowly into Pearl Harbor. It was the first time the harbor had seen a visit by a Chinese warship.

The warship was named after the great Chinese navigator Zheng He. More than 600 years before, he had led a then-massive exploration fleet seven times to the Indian Ocean (called the "West Ocean" by the Chinese), and he had visited more than 30 countries and regions around the world. This famed sailor set a great example for friendly visits between China and other countries and in so doing wrote a glorious chapter in the history of global navigation.

The *Zhenghe* had sailed from Qinghai on March 31. On the morning of April 4, after crossing the International Date Line, it became the first Chinese naval vessel to enter the Western Hemisphere. On April 10, the *Zhenghe* rendezvoused in the open sea with the welcoming U.S. guided missile destroyer *Ingersoll*.

And so in the second week of April, 1989, with the red wreath of friendship hanging from its bow, the *Zhenghe* sailed beside the *Ingersoll* into Pearl Harbor to a 21-gun salute. Once the U.S. warship was at anchor in the harbor, its crew in formation saluted the Chinese warships. The U.S Pacific Fleet commander, Admiral David Jeremiah, the Pacific Fleet Marine Force commander, Lieutenant General Godfrey, the USN Third Fleet commander, Vice Admiral David Dorsett, Hawaii Governor John D. Waihee III and locals from all walks of life, along with representatives of the Chinese community, were at the harbor to

The U.S Pacific Fleet commander, Admiral David Jeremiah, welcoming the visiting *Zhenghe*

welcome the warship. That night, Admiral Jeremiah hosted a banquet at his home for his Chinese guests.

To show their appreciation for the hospitality of the United States, the Chinese Navy's Theatrical Performance Team put on a show for U.S. military personnel, the representatives of the Chinese community, members of the Pearl Harbor sailor's club and locals from Waikiki Beach Park.

On April 18, the *Zhenghe*'s amicable visit to Pearl Harbor ended a great success and the ship set sail for home.

The occasion of a single Chinese ship crossing the Pacific and sailing into Hawaii after 12 days and nights at sea prompted overwhelming local response. According to Admiral Jeremiah, the Chinese Navy was now able to carry out oceangoing missions and could become a "blue water navy." Local Hawaiian newspapers and TV stations reported the visit of the warship in their news highlights. At the time, as well, Chinese émigrés were celebrating the 200th anniversary of their emigration to

8. THE COURSE OF FRIENDSHIP

Hawaii. When referring to the significance of the Chinese visit, Governor Waihee noted that the visit gave a boost to the anniversary activities. The ship's visit was not only a big event for the entire Chinese community but also for the state of Hawaii.

Since that time the *Zhenghe* has paid many overseas visits as the Peace Emissary of the Chinese Navy. The first special ocean training ship made by China, it entered service in April 1987. Between then and April 2012, the ship sailed over 280,000 nautical miles. In sum, in its 25 years of service to that point, the *Zhenghe* sailed to ports in more than 30 countries around the world and became an important window for foreign exchanges by the Chinese Navy.

On April 16, 2012, the *Zhenghe*, commanded by Deputy Chief of Staff Liao Shining, set sail from Lvshun on a voyage around the world, the second around-the-world trip for a PLAN vessel. Onboard personnel were more than 300 officers and men of the Chinese Navy, and the Navy cadets came from 13 countries. The plan was to sail more than 30,000 nautical miles in five months and visit Vietnam, Malaysia, India, Italy, Spain, Canada, Ecuador, Polynesia, Tonga, Indonesia and Brunei. During this voyage, the ship would dock at Djibouti, Jamaica and Australia.

PLAN'S FIRST TRIP AROUND THE WORLD

In 2002, the missile destroyer *Qingdao* and the comprehensive depot ship *Taicang* (now the *Hongzehu*), carrying 506 officers and men, paid visits by invitation to 10 ports in 10 countries, including Singapore, Egypt, Turkey, Ukraine, Greece, Portugal, Brazil, Ecuador, Peru and French Polynesia. To undertake such an operation was symbolic of the goodwill of the Chinese people and their Navy.

The visiting formation set sail from the beautiful northern city of Qingdao on May 15. On May 23, the ships arrived at Singapore and docked at the port of Changi. After leaving Singapore on May 27, the ships passed through the Strait of Malacca, crossed the Indian Ocean, crossed the Red Sea and passed through the Suez Canal. They arrived

Casting float bottles near the Equator in the Atlantic

in Alexandria, Egypt, on June 14, and after five days they left Egypt. They then visited the Turkish port of Akcansa Ambarli, the port of Sevastopol in Ukraine, the port of Piraeus in Athens, Greece, and the port of Lisbon, Spain. On July 14, the ships started across the Atlantic Ocean for South America. They arrived at the port of Fortaleza, Brazil, on the morning on July 23, then sailed to Guayaquil, Ecuador, the port of Callao, in Peru, and Papeete in French Polynesia. On September 3, after the visit to French Polynesia, the ships crossed the Pacific Ocean in the north and returned to their starting point, Qingdao.

This around-the-world voyage took 132 days and involved 33,000 nautical miles. The ships sailed across the Indian Ocean, the Atlantic and the Pacific. The sailors travelled across Asia, Africa, Europe, North America, South America and Oceania. They passed through 15 straits and channels, across 22 bays or gulfs, by 45 islands and at 68 latitudes. They crossed the equator six times and were able to avoid rough seas and strong or low-pressure cyclone conditions seven times. This accomplishment filled in a gap for the Chinese in world naval history.

8. THE COURSE OF FRIENDSHIP

During each docking period at the various ports, the ships held a deck reception party. In Egypt, ambassadors from 14 countries and envoys to Egypt from 10 countries attended. Meanwhile, the ships were also available for visits by citizens. At the port of Fortaleza, in Brazil, the visitors line was a mile long. More than 30,000 people visited the ships. At this port there was a woman selling seashells. Before the Chinese warships left, she told the Chinese officers through an interpreter, "The sailors on your warships go running and work out every day and you also clean up. Our port has never been so clean and tidy."

During the warships' docking at the port of Lisbon, Spain, the Chinese sailors wanted to use a local magnetic card phone. At first, security officers denied the request with a smile. But after observing the Chinese for two days, the visitors were invited to use the phone and to feel free to call their friends and relatives. The security guards explained their change in attitude: "We [two] used to do security for many foreign vessels and warships. There were 38 ships here last year alone. There's always somebody causing trouble, like refusing to pay after taking a taxi, or creating a disturbance after drinking. But you officers and men are so well behaved. And you are so disciplined. We hope you will come again."

Among the personnel of the Chinese Navy Global Voyage Vessels Formation, the four poised and self-assured female cadets were particularly striking. No matter where their ships docked, their presence always attracted the interest of the locals. Everywhere, the four impressed with their graceful manner and professional demeanor. For example, during the visit to Egypt, the Chinese Embassy held a welcome banquet in Alexandria, and important members of Egyptian society and envoys from each country were invited to attend. During the banquet, Hao Kun had the attention of all present with a beautiful Chinese zither performance. Afterward, the spouses of many envoys surrounded Hao Kun and asked her to teach them how to play the instrument. The wife of the Finnish diplomatic envoy even danced to Hao Kun's zither.

On June 25, the Chinese Navy Global Voyage Vessels Formation arrived at Sevastopol in the south Crimean Peninsula. In this famous city of heroes, the statues and monuments everywhere speak of its glorious past. Admiral Yezhelev, commander-in-chief of the Ukraine

Navy, attended a banquet held for him on the *Qingdao* by commander Ding Yiping.

The admiral liked the exquisite dishes very much. He was surprised to know that the dish called "fruit and vegetable carving" was made of carrots and white radishes, and he was so impressed with the traditional Chinese culinary arts that he asked to see the chef, 29-year-old sergeant Wu Zhiliang.

Soon after, Wu Zhiliang came to the admiral's table with a knife in one hand and a large turnip in the other. In only a few minutes, he had carved a delicate dove from the turnip, which he then presented to the admiral. Yezhelev hugged him and gave him a thumbs-up. He also proposed a toast and praised the chef as the best soldier in the Chinese army.

The admiral said, "In Ukraine, a general is charged with promoting a soldier who performs with such outstanding ability. This soldier who can make such delicate artwork should be promoted immediately." He asked Ding, "Do you have the authority to promote him?" The commander nodded and smiled, but said, "If I promoted him every time we arrived in a new country, he would be my leader by the end of this voyage!"

In Brazil, a country that loves soccer, the Chinese and Brazilian navies played a game in the port of Fortaleza. The Chinese team comprised

Brazilians waiting to board the Chinese warships at Fortaleza, Brazil

men from the *Qingdao* and the *Taicang* who were interested in soccer. The Brazilian Navy Sailors Training School team consisted of students and staff. The Brazilians had won many matches with other navy soccer teams from Europe and the United States.

At about 4:00 that afternoon the match began. The Brazilians chose the common 4-4-2 formation, and the Chinese the 5-4-1. The Brazilians shot at the Chinese goal with quick-footed maneuvers and perfect coordination. Soon after the start of the match, they had almost gained control of the situation. But the Chinese players weren't daunted and played tougher as the match went on. There was a huge crowd in the auditorium—cheerleading squads danced the samba and cheered for the players on both sides. When the game ended, it was a 1-1 draw.

This global voyage by the Chinese Navy Vessels Formation was unprecedented in the history of the Chinese Navy.

HARMONIOUS WALTZES AT SEA

White ceremonial uniform, blue shawl, well-proportioned physique, professional performance—this is the young musician of the PLAN Military Band, the pride of the Navy. The band often makes visits abroad. When making long sails on the vast ocean to foreign countries, the band gives small-scale concerts on deck for the sailors to recover from fatigue. And wherever the visiting formation goes, band members perform as messengers of friendship. Music bridges the gap between hearts. It can help overcome the barriers of languages and nations. It can make strangers feel closer.

Music expresses sentiments beyond words and reaches into the heart to touch what is universal in all of us. It is the ligament of peacekeeping. The world's military bands bring with them sincere signals of harmony and friendship.

Established in 1986, the Chinese Navy Military Band is known these days around the world. It has visited many countries with the Visiting Formation and has given hundreds of performances for military personnel and civilians around the world. It has done exchange concerts

In 1998, the Chinese warship formation first visited Oceania. This was the first time the Chinese Navy Military Band performed at the Sydney Opera House.

and joint performances with more than 20 military bands, from the United States, Russia, the United Kingdom, Germany, Italy, Australia and elsewhere.

On the evening of June 20, 2002, at the Peace Plaza at Aksaz Naval Base in Turkey, the audience rose and danced with joy to the PLAN Military Band's rendition of the Turkish folk song "Alas, my youth!" This scene of harmony and joy was once novel for the young sailors in the band. Now it is the norm.

The performances given by the PLAN Military Band show off the members' unique skills. While playing instruments, they also march, presenting the audiences with both the spectacular visual and artistic enjoyment. And each time they're rewarded with enthusiastic applause.

In 1997, the PLAN Military Band visited Hawaii aboard visiting Chinese warships. On the day they arrived, the band went to the post of the Military Band of the U.S. Pacific Fleet and rehearsed with them. Eleven years before, in 1986, when visiting China for the first time, musicians of the U.S. Pacific Fleet had performed with the PLAN Military Band, which had been formed only eight months before.

On March 11, 1997, the military bands of the Chinese and U.S. navies gave plaza concerts and did a joint performance of "Hands Across the Sea." The two bands played together under two conductors like a seamless heavenly robe. The performance won raves. Admiral Archie Clemins, commander of the Pacific Fleet, went onstage to compliment the musicians.

In April 1998, the PLAN Military Band performed jointly with the Royal New Zealand Navy Band, and again their performance was a great success. During the farewell dinner afterward, the Royal New Zealand Navy Band played the New Zealand song "Goodbye" in farewell to guests who had come a long way to visit. The song evoked a warm response from the musicians of the Chinese Navy, who then played "Auld Lang Syne." Deeply affected by the music, strangers in the audience hugged like old friends.

On a visit to the Philippines, the People's naval formation personnel were invited to attend a reception at the Chinese Embassy to welcome military officers from different countries. Philippine Vice Admiral Eduardo Santos had planned to attend for only 10 minutes, but when the Chinese Navy Military Band had performed just one piece of music, Santos raised his glass to conductor Li Xing and said happily, "Your band is the best I've ever seen. I was really fascinated by the music you played. I've decided to put off my meeting and stay for your performance!" The dinner party lasted a while, and Santos was bursting with energy and in high spirits the entire time.

"Wish for our warships to be arks of peace. Pray for a world without war." These are the hope of the Military Band of the Chinese Navy, and so "Auld Lang Syne" is one of the songs they love most. The band chooses this beautiful and lyrical piece almost every time for a perfect end to a performance, because this song is an embodiment of the basic principle of China's Navy: to promote world peace and friendship.

Port Calls by Foreign Navies

As messengers of friendship, visiting warships are an important means of diplomacy. While the Chinese Navy has dispatched more and more warships to visit other countries, it has invited even more foreign warships to pay return visits. In over 60 years, more than 300 warships and other navy vessels from more than 50 countries have called on Shanghai, Qingdao, Zhanjiang, Guangzhou and other Chinese port cities, and this has greatly enhanced the friendships between China and these countries.

THE SOVIET FLEET'S FIRST VISIT TO SHANGHAI

From June 20 to 26, 1956, the Soviet Pacific Fleet visited Shanghai at the invitation of the Chinese government. This was the first time the PRC received a foreign naval contingent. Commanded by Vice-Admiral Valentin Andreevich Chekurov, the Soviet fleet included the cruiser *Dmitri Pozharski*, the destroyers *Wisdom* and *Enlighten* and 2,183 officers and men. These three warships, built in the early 1950s by the Soviet Union, were state-of-the art at the time.

Originally a Japanese warship, the *Nanchang* of the 6th Frigate Detachment was assigned to welcome the Soviets. After the Anti-Japanese War, the ship had been taken over by the KMT Navy. In September 1949, the men on the ship defected and surrendered to the PLA. After repairs at the Jiangnan Shipyard, the *Nanchang* was incorporated into the ESF. Back then it was considered the best ship in the PLAN fleet.

On the morning of June 20, 1956, the *Nanchang* sailed from Wusong Port. At dawn, the ship's radar located a Soviet cruiser. The two boats rapidly approached, and when only 20 chains separated them, the *Nanchang* warship fired a 19-gun salute and the signalmen sent the message, "Welcome, and congratulations on your smooth arrival." The flagship of the Soviet formation fired a 19-gun salute in return. There was a loud "Hurrah" on both vessels.

At about 6 a.m., the deputy commander of the ESF, Peng Deqing, and other personnel took torpedo boats to the Soviet flagship, cruiser *Dmitri Pozharski*. Commander Chekurov was on deck to welcome them when they boarded. Soon after, with the *Nanchang* in the lead, the *Wisdom* and the *Enlighten* sailed across the Yangtze River Estuary into the Huangpu River.

8. THE COURSE OF FRIENDSHIP

On the afternoon of June 20, the Chinese Navy commander General Xiao Jingguang, who had come to Shanghai especially for the event, boarded the *Dmitri Pozharski*. He reviewed the Soviet Honor Guard to the sound of martial music. Commander Chekurov then hosted a banquet for him and conferred an honorary degree on him on behalf of the Leningrad Military and Political Academy, where Xiao had studied for two years.

Later, four generals from the Soviet fleet arrived in Beijing on a charter flight accompanied by Deputy Commander Peng. They were received by then- Secretary of National Defense Marshal Peng Dehuai and former premier Zhou Enlai. The Shanghai Municipal Government and the ESF provided the Soviet representatives with Chinese handicrafts. The soldiers received pens and watches as gifts—considered "luxuries" in China at the time. They loved their gifts so much it was hard for them to put them down.

During this visit, China and the Soviet Union took part in marvelous interactive activities. The Shanghai government hosted a welcome

Commander Xiao Jingguang touring a visiting Soviet warship

meeting, garden parties and celebration parties. More than 13,000 soldiers and civilians participated, and more than 6,000 were invited to board the Soviet warships and take a look around. The Soviet soldiers and civilians were invited to visit 19 Chinese entities, including warships, factories, schools and agricultural cooperatives. Some of the Soviets also visited Hangzhou, in Zhejiang Province, and other scenic spots. The Soviet fleet's Chorus Group gave three theatrical performances in Shanghai, and local artists presented traditional Chinese operas, music, acrobatics and more than 100 other programs. The Soviet guests were invited to film showings. There were also friendly football, basketball and volleyball games.

Now it happens that on the morning of June 20, when the Soviet warships were sailing into Shanghai, an employee at Shanghai's Army Hospital, Xia Guizhi, was giving birth to twin boys. Her husband, Wang Jianguo, was one of the locals responsible for receiving the Soviets. To commemorate the coming of the two Soviet ships, this couple named their twins Zhi Mou (Wisdom) and Qi Meng (Enlighten).

When Prochenko, chief Soviet advisor to the ESF, and Vice-Admiral Chekurov heard the story, they were pleased. They said, "The names of our destroyers have become the names of two little citizens of Shanghai. What a great honor!" The captains of the *Wisdom* and the *Enlighten* along with six sailors visited the newborn boys in the hospital. They said, "They are two little sailors of our warships!" and gave the children baby clothes and toys.

U.S. WARSHIP VISITS QINGDAO

On November 5, 1986, the destroyer *Reeves*, the destroyer *Oldendorf* and the frigate *Renzi*, under Admiral James Lyons, then-commander of the U.S Pacific Fleet, arrived at Qingdao. It was the first time U.S. warships visited the PRC.

Liu Huaqing, commander of the Chinese Navy, hosted a banquet for Lyons and other officers at the hotel in Qingdao, where he recited a famous line by Confucius, "Is it not a delight after all to have friends

8. THE COURSE OF FRIENDSHIP

Commander Liu Huaqing and others reviewing the U.S. warships' guard of honor accompanied by Admiral James Lyons, commander of the U.S Pacific Fleet

come from afar?" Lyons grasped the meaning and repeatedly expressed gratitude to his host.

Chinese and U.S. personnel visited each other's warships, and U.S. representatives visited the Chinese Navy Submarine College. The Art Troupe of the Chinese Navy's Political Department and the U.S. Warships Military Band gave a joint performance in the Great Hall of the People, in Qingdao, and sailors from both countries also played several friendly games of football and basketball.

Nearly 3,000 U.S sailors were invited to Tsingtao Brewery. The factory director made a welcome speech and gave some of the history of the factory. Before he could finish, though, the Americans couldn't resist the temptation of the beer. They drank freely and happily, and asked several times for the beer-drinking time to be extended. A sailor exclaimed as he left the brewery, "This is awesome!"

On November 11, the six-day U.S. visit to Qingdao was over. That morning, Qingdao held a grand send-off ceremony, after which the three U.S. warships sailed out of Qingdao behind the Chinese destroyer *Dalian*.

Joint Military Exercises

On October 21, 2003, near the port of Shanghai, Chinese warships, seaplanes and helicopters held a joint military parade with the visiting Pakistani destroyer *Babur* and the comprehensive depot ship *Nasr*. This was the first time the PLAN conducted a joint military exercise with a foreign naval force. Since then, the number of joint military exercises conducted by China and other nations has grown significantly, to the point that the joint exercise has become an important form of military exchange between China and other countries.

THE FIRST SINO-FRENCH JOINT NAVAL EFFORT

On March 16, 2004, in the Yellow Sea near Qingdao, China's guided-missile destroyer *Harbin* and the comprehensive depot ship *Hongzehu* received a sudden distress signal, "Fire!" from the French warship *Commandant Birot*. The *Harbin* went immediately to the distressed ship and found smoke billowing. Two Chinese shipborne helicopters took to the skies over the *Commandant Birot* and arranged to rescue the injured. The *Harbin* put down life rafts, and eight marines, three wearing silver-gray firefighting suits, sailed to the French ship to fight the fire and rescue the injured.

And so played out the scene of the first Sino-French joint military maritime effort.

Four days earlier, on March 12, to commemorate the fortieth anniversary of diplomatic relations between France and China, the French Navy had dispatched a formation that included the antisubmarine destroyer *Latouche-Treville* and the light frigate *Commandant Birot* and more than 700 personnel for a visit to Qingdao. It was during during their return voyage that the naval forces of the two countries conducted joint exercises outside Qingdao.

At about 8:00 a.m., the sirens of the *Harbin* blared as the ship guided the French formation out of the port of Qingdao into open waters. The warships first performed communication exercises with semaphore

8. THE COURSE OF FRIENDSHIP

and colored light signals and then did a formation navigation exercise.

Around 1:20 p.m., a French Navy Lynx helicopter landed on the deck of the *Harbin*, and a Chinese helicopter landed on the French warship. This was the first maritime landing of one country's navy helicopter on the warship of another.

Firefighting exercise

Before landing, the two helicopters performed altitude conversions and an aerial photo exchange. Then they did maritime supply exercises. The *Harbin*, the *Latouche-Treville* and the *Commandant Birot* sailed around the *Hongzehu* in a close-triangle formation. For its part, the *Hongzehu* conducted a simulation training of three warships supplying simultaneously and a single warship supplying. Given that this supply procedure can extend a nation's maritime fighting capability, this joint effort was important. And it was the first time the Chinese Navy conducted such a joint exercise with a foreign naval force from coastal waters to off-lying seas.

A firefighting drill was the last exercise in the series of the first Sino-French maritime military exercises. At 5:25 p.m., the exercises were concluded, and the Chinese sailors lined up on their ships to wave farewell to the French sailors with whom they had drilled that day.

JOINT SEARCH AND RESCUE BY THE CHINESE AND U.S. NAVIES

On a lovely fall day in 2006, a new chapter was begun in the history of communication between the Chinese and U.S. navies.

From 11:00 a.m. to 4:10 p.m. Pacific time, on September 20, a visiting Chinese warship formation conducted a joint maritime search-and-rescue exercise with the U.S. Navy near the San Diego, California, harbor.

Light communications exercise between Chinese and U.S. warships

This was the first time the navies of these two countries worked together in a joint exercise. The scenario was that a U.S. vessel, having met with a mishap off the U.S. West Coast, would be missing for five hours, and Chinese vessels passing through would be asked to help with the search.

The exercise began in the morning. At 1:35 p.m., the U.S. command reported, "A U.S. ship is in distress in the sea, near XX degrees north, XX degrees west. We ask the Chinese warships to work with the guided-missile destroyer USS *Shoup* and Seahawk helicopters in a joint search. If you find the target, please guide it immediately."

"From the *Qingdao*, roger!"

"Roger!" "Roger!" Came the high-frequency telephone responses from the U.S. helicopter unit and the USS *Shoup*. After receiving the request, the Chinese and U.S. warships rapidly formed a search formation.

The antennae of the shipborne search radar on the searching ships began to turn. In the air, meanwhile, one shipborne helicopter from each nation was also searching.

Half an hour later the helicopters detected their objective at nearly

8. THE COURSE OF FRIENDSHIP

the same time. After being briefed, the *Qingdao* and the USS *Shoup* adjusted course and sailed toward their objective at full speed.

In less than an hour, the warships of both nations were in the right place for rescue teams to coordinate efforts in the rescue of the ship and the injured. A fire was put out, and the injured were moved in minutes.

When the search-and-rescue operation was concluded, the U.S. commander and the captain of Squadron 7 of the U.S. Pacific Fleet and some U.S. combat and navigation officers boarded the *Qingdao* to evaluate the exercise.

The U.S. captain said, "During this exercise we witnessed the fantastic, amazing professional skill of China's sailors. The U.S. and Chinese warships coordinated seamlessly and showed good combination. Through such teamwork I feel confident that the United States and China will conduct joint search-and-rescue missions in the future."

The commander of the Chinese Navy Visiting Warship Formation, Rear Admiral Wang Fushan, sent a telegram to the Commander of the U.S. Navy Pacific Fleet, Admiral Gary Roughead. He said, "The cooperation between our two nations was very pleasant. The commanding skills and professional quality of the U.S. Pacific Fleet impressed us deeply."

Two months later, another search-and-rescue mission took place in the South China Sea, and here the Chinese and U.S. navies conducted a joint exercise in Chinese waters for the first time. This second-stage exercise was deeper than the first, which meant that the two navies had made substantial progress in non-traditional security cooperation.

This exercise was held after the amphibious transport dock landing ship *Juno*, commanded by Roughead and manned by 650, finished a friendly visit to Zhanjiang, Guangdong Province. The *Juno*, the U.S. guided-missile destroyer *Fitzgerald*, China's guided-missile destroyer *Zhanjiang* (on standby in these waters) and China's comprehensive depot ship *Dongtinghu* participated, along with fixed-wing aircraft from both nations.

The exercise was in four parts: a communications exercise, a maritime warship rendezvous, a warship formation maneuver and a joint maritime search-and-rescue operation. The scenario here was that a merchant ship would disappear after sailing for three days in the South

China Sea. The Chinese would ask a passing U.S. warship to assist in a search, and in a rescue if needed.

Just as with the first search/rescue exercise, the U.S. and Chinese worked in close coordination, and their communications went smoothly. The mission was accomplished.

Then-vice director of the Foreign Affairs Office of China's Ministry of Defense, Rear Admiral Qian Lihua, said after observing this maritime exercise, "The Chinese and U.S. naval officers and men showed a high-quality, advanced level of professionalism and team spirit. This lays a foundation for further cooperation and communication in other areas."

THE SINO-BRITISH FRIENDSHIP 2007 JOINT MILITARY EXERCISE

It was 1:50 p.m., September 10, 2007, on the Atlantic.

The guided-missile destroyer *Guangzhou*, flying the Chinese flag, and the British aircraft carrier *Ark Royal*, flying the British flag, were sailing side-by-side through wind and waves toward the area designated for the Sino-British Friendship 2007 joint military exercise.

The scenario for this exercise was that a ship from the country, X, would meet with a mishap and cabins were on fire. There were dead and injured on board, and the ship was in dire need of rescue. At the request of X government, the Chinese and British Navy fleet formations would sail rapidly to search for the ship. The Chinese and British officers would alternate command at different stages of the operation.

And so at 2:00 p.m., the two vessels set out in the same direction at the same speed, with just five chains between them. While this was happening, Staff Sergeant Zhang Lingsheng, aboard the *Guangzhou*, used light signals to send a first set of codes to the British aircraft carrier. Several sets of light codes followed from the warships of both nations and "spoke" plainly via high-frequency radio waves and the ships communicated successfully.

The climax occurred during the joint search-and-rescue phase of the operation. By 2:30, the Chinese comprehensive depot ship *Weishanhu*,

8. THE COURSE OF FRIENDSHIP

In September 2007, Chinese warships conduct a joint exercise with a British aircraft carrier

simulating the damaged ship from X that had lost contact with others, had drifted to point Y. The *Ark Royal* and the *Guangzhou*, commanded by the British, moved to designated areas for the search-and-rescue phase of the operation. When they found the "distressed" ship, they reported to the British. Then the British handed over command to the Chinese. At this point the *Guangzhou*, the *Ark Royal* and the *Weishanhu* formed a triangle, and a British Navy Lynx helicopter, which had flown to the scene from the Navy Base at Portsmouth, hovered overhead to boost morale. The formation was a magnificent picture of a solid maritime military exercise.

At 2:30, the Chinese commander ordered the *Guangzhou* and the *Ark Royal* to drop boats. The *Guangzhou* dispatched its deputy engineer commander, Zheng Qingyu, and eight rescuers in orange lifejackets. Rubber boats were sent out by the British aircraft carrier, and the navy rescuers from the two ships rapidly climbed rescue ladders and landed on the "damaged" ship for the emergency rescue. Within 20 minutes, the mission was accomplished.

This joint exercise was the first time the Chinese Navy conducted a joint military exercise with an aircraft carrier from another nation.

PEACE 2009 MULTINATIONAL NAVAL EXERCISE

The at-sea phase of the Aman 2009 (*aman* is an Urdu word for *peace*) multinational naval exercise began at 6:30 a.m. on March 9, 2009, when warships and other vessels of several countries set sail in formation from Karachi, Pakistan. One by one, 11 ships crossed simulated minefields to reach the drill area at sea. The participating warships included the destroyers *Guangzhou*, *Tariq*, *Tippu Sultan* and *Badr*; the Pakistani comprehensive depot ship *Nasser*; the U.S. cruiser *Lake Champlain* and the frigate *Porterfield*; the British Navy frigate *Portland* and oil tanker *Wave Night*; the Australian frigate *Warramunga*; the Malaysian Navy patrol boat *Kedah*; and the Bangladesh Navy frigate *Abu Bakr*.

At 2:40 p.m., the warships began performing maneuvers in formation, including a column-formation conversion exercise. At 3:40, helicopter deck landings began. China's Z-9 shipborne helicopters took off smoothly and after flying more than 20 nautical miles landed twice on the British Royal Navy's *Portland*, while a British Royal Navy *Lynx* was able to land on the deck of the *Guangzhou*. U.S. Sea Hawks, Royal Australian Navy *Sea Hawks* and a Pakistan Navy *Skylark* also did deck landings on ships not of their navies.

The formation, including China's *Guangzhou* and the U.S. cruiser *Lake Champlain*, participating in the Peace 2009 multinational naval exercise

8. THE COURSE OF FRIENDSHIP

At 5:45, floating-target firing practice began. To the rapid siren blasts that signal combat alert, the *Guangzhou* fired a main gun. With a thunderous roar, the first fire hit and sank a floating target 3.5 nautical miles away, which meant great success in the most important exercise for *Guangzhou* during this drill, a firing at sea and an achieved objective. The commander of the lead ship, the *Portland*, sent a congratulatory telegram to the *Guangzhou* for an "awesome job."

THE MARITIME COOPERATION 2012 SINO-RUSSIAN JOINT EXERCISE

In the spring of 2012, a Chinese "merchant ship" on the Yellow Sea was boarded by 10 armed "hijackers."

A joint convoy formation immediately dispatched warships to the site. In five minutes, 20 special combat soldiers from the Chinese and Russian navies were moving at high speed in four boats toward the flanks of the "hijacked" ship. Under cover of fire from the air, they climbed aboard, coordinated efforts and quickly brought the "hijackers" under control. Soon after, they were able to "rescue" the ship's crew.

This was a planned scenario in the Maritime Cooperation 2012 Sino-Russian joint exercise, held near Qingdao from April 22 to 27, 2012. In this pioneering cooperative effort, there were 23 warships, two submarines, 13 fixed-wing aircraft, nine helicopters and two special combat units. Of these, there were seven Russian surface ships and four helicopters, and 20 Russian marines. The exercises involved mid-air, water surface and underwater scenarios. In harsh weather, the Russians and Chinese worked in close coordination. All the drills were done in one stretch.

The cooperation came not only from mutual identification with strategic interests and the two nations being of one mind but also from emotional bonding.

In the six days allotted for the joint exercises, the two countries held colorful activities including sampan contests, basketball games, football matches and a special operation performance. On April 23, on the

The Sino-Russian joint naval exercise

sixty-third anniversary of the founding of the Chinese Navy, the Russian warships flew China's national flag. The Russians even prepared excellent programs in celebration of the Chinese Navy's birthday.

In the seven years after the 2005 Sino-Russian joint military exercise, including multinational naval activity in 2009 and the 2012 Sino-Russian joint exercise, the Chinese and Russian navies worked together many times in friendship, harmony and cooperation.

The Russian commander and naval deputy of chief of staff Rear Admiral Leonid Sukhanov pointed out, "The drills, including joint escort, joint search- and-rescue and joint antihijacking were all done so both nations could gain rich experience in maintaining regional security and stability."

The Chinese Naval Cadets Week International

In 1990, the United States' West Point Military Academy established a program. Every March, the Academy arranges for cadets to visit more than 30 colleges and academies around the world. In April, West Point

8. THE COURSE OF FRIENDSHIP

invites representatives of foreign military colleges and academies where the U.S. cadets will be visiting to participate in weeklong activities at the Academy. The event is called International Cadets Week.

In 2009, the First International Cadets Week Activity for the Chinese Navy was unveiled at the PLAN's Dalian Warship Academy. Eight cadets from the military colleges and academies of Germany, Japan and Korea were invited to participate. The following week, the foreign cadets and 16 students at the Dalian Warship Academy lived, studied and trained together.

On June 25, 2012, the Second International Cadets Week Activity was held at Dalian Warship Academy, and this proved to be even more colorful than the first. Eighteen navy cadets from nine countries and 34 Chinese cadets were made a team, and they lived, studied and trained together. The team watched briefing videos, visited the central lab, planetarium and simulation training center, and they observed formation training of Dalian Warship Academy cadets. The participants were also schooled in sailing and on sampans and trained in armed cross-country running and steeplechase. In their leisure hours, they went sightseeing around Dalian.

In the presentations by the Chinese and foreign cadets on June 26, the students from 10 countries showed slides and videos and played music, among other forms of expressions. After each presentation, there was ardent discussion and interaction.

In addition to this formal occasion for communication, the cadets exchanged ideas and had in-depth discussions. "Despite our differences in various aspects, as young men we have in common a lot of interests and hobbies," Chinese cadet Fan Yuan said. "We covered a spectrum of issues and topics in our chats, from hometowns and upbringing to course subject matter and teaching methods at naval colleges and academies. We even talked about the different historical and cultural backgrounds of our countries, as well as the ongoing European Cup matches."

Chinese and foreign students working together

So while there was a collision of ideas

and ways of thinking, the cultures of different countries were blending. For the foreign cadets who traveled to Dalian, the ancient and mysterious nation of China was full of charm and glamour.

On the afternoon on June 26, an Australian Defense Force Academy cadet along with 17 cadets from other nations learned the martial art of Taijiquan, which has a long history. Although a little awkward, the Australian practiced. "In Sydney, Australia, Chinese seniors often do Taijiquan in parks. Watching the slow pace and movements, I've always been curious," he said. "Now, after doing Taijiquan myself, I find it very pleasant. I feel totally relaxed after doing it."

So foreign cadets could learn more about and experience Chinese culture, Dalian Warship Academy organized visits to the homes of a Chinese instructor. To welcome his guests coming from afar, the professor in the Department of Navigation, Li Tianwei, prepared activities for a day at home. How to teach the foreign students more about Chinese culture? Li Tianwei's choices were tea and dumplings.

"This is my first time in close contact with a Chinese family. I love the ambiance of the Chinese family; it's intimate and harmonious. I'd heard that the Chinese are friendly and hospitable. When I came to this home in Dalian, I learned from my own experience how friendly they are," reported another Australian cadet.

And according to an Italian cadet from Livorno, such cultural exchanges and communication are significant. "This kind of activity can boost mutual understanding, which can keep conflict and war away from our planet."

A Naval Carnival in Qingdao

In north China there is a beautiful harbor. The water is wide and deep. The harbor is like a bottle, with a small neck and a large body. The wind is fair and the sea is calm here, and this is where the 2008 Summer Olympics sailing event was held.

In April 2009, though, foggy and rainy weather blurred sky and sea into one indistinct color for a couple of days. Then, on the evening of

8. THE COURSE OF FRIENDSHIP

April 18, a Mexican Navy training ship, an ARM Cuauhtémoc BE-01, suddenly appeared out of the mist. The people on the dock became excited. The scenic port of Qingdao was about to receive its first "guest," who would participate in the multinational naval activities celebrating the sixtieth anniversary of the founding of the PLAN.

In the two days following, various warships and other navy vessels gathered at Qingdao. These included the gigantic Russian guided-missile destroyer *Varyag*, the advanced U.S. guided-missile destroyer *Fitzgerald*, the Canadian comprehensive depot ship *Protecteur*, the Australian patrol boat *Pirie* (with a displacement of only 298 tons), the South Korean guided-missile destroyer *Kang Gam Chan* (planning to fight piracy in Somalia) and the Indian guided-missile destroyer INS *Mumbai*. Qingdao was welcoming a truly international warship contingent.

On the afternoon of April 20, the South Korean KDX-II amphibious assault ship *Dokdo* arrived at Qingdao. This ship, the last to arrive, had the largest displacement of those participating in the celebration. In all, to celebrate the sixtieth anniversary of the founding of the PLAN, 29 naval delegations and 21 warships from 14 countries were invited to participate in the multinational activities at Qingdao. (Along with the ships came helicopters.)

Several hours after the *Dokdo* docked, PLAN commander Wu Shengli declared the celebration of the sixtieth anniversary of the founding of the PLAN officially begun.

"THE CHINESE NAVY IS AMAZING!"

On the morning of April 22, 2009, officers and naval delegates from 29 countries were invited to visit the port of Qingdao. They looked with great interest at the Chinese naval vessels docked there. The guided-missile destroyer *Wenzhou*, the conventionally powered submarine Great Wall 218 and hospital ship *Peace Ark* had been designed and made in China. They had come into service only recently and represented the latest developments in Chinese naval equipment.

The *Wenzhou* was one of the newest PLAN guided-missile frigates.

It had a full-load displacement of 4,400 tons and had entered service in September 2005. As one of the PLAN's frigates with the best information technology, it has strong antiaircraft, antiship and antisubmarine capabilities. Stealth technology is also in use in this vessel. The *Wenzhou* has a cruising range of more than 4,000 nautical miles, and its self-supplying capability can last as long as 15 days and nights.

The conventionally powered submarine, *Great Wall 218*, is a second-generation domestically designed and manufactured torpedo attack submarine. It is also one of the most important submarines in active service in the Chinese Navy. Its performance is among the most advanced in the world. It is designed mainly for coastal defense, and for antiship and antisubmarine combat.

The *Peace Ark* hospital ship is specially designed to provide maritime medical care and treatment. It came into use in 2008, and the standard of medical care equals that of a Third Class A-Level hospital. Its entry into China's naval force was a great step forward in the Navy's maritime medical support capability. On hearing brief introductions by hospital ship personnel, one U.S. officer said, "The medical team members of the PLAN have a high degree of medical skill. This Chinese naval hospital ship will not be outmoded in 10 years. I truly hope the Chinese medical team members and the medical personnel on the U.S. Navy hospital ship will exchange visits at regular intervals in order to carry out the common mission of international humanitarian assistance."

The Chilean Navy commander, Admiral Rodolfo Codina Diaz, also spoke highly of the *Peace Ark*. He even called over Chinese journalists and photographers nearby to commemorate this wonderful time at the *Peace Ark*.

The personnel on the three Chinese vessels warmly received the visitors. Commander Xu Xianhong, who had been to Russia for further education, introduced the functions of each ship in fluent English. The visitors asked things like, "What kind of antiaircraft missiles does the frigate use?" "What is the range of the shipborne guns?" and "How many days does this ship sail each year?" Xu Xianhong smiled and commented, "Many officers and men speak English fluently. They embody confidence and the pride of taking to the naval profession."

8. THE COURSE OF FRIENDSHIP

Embarking on the warship to visit Visiting a warship

After visiting the *Wenzhou*, the commander of Canadian Maritime Forces Pacific (known as Royal Canadian Navy's Pacific Fleet), Rear Admiral Tyrone Pile, remarked, "I boarded Chinese ships in 1988 and felt acutely the rapid growth and development of the Chinese Navy. I hope I'll have more opportunities to cooperate with such a fleet so we can meet collectively all kinds of threats at sea."

Because of the narrow access way, three groups were formed to visit the conventionally powered submarine *Great Wall 218*. Captain Bu Renyong spoke with the visitors and guided them into each area. Captain Bu, who himself has visited naval forces in many countries, said, "I've learned a lot by communicating with foreign navy officers and sailors. Such experiences not only help us understand the latest developments in other countries, they also broaden our own horizons and change our ways of thinking."

After seeing the three vessels, many of the other visitors made comments. Indonesian Navy Chief of Staff Admiral Sumar Dijono expressed deep feelings about the development of the Chinese Navy. To this point he had visited China and its warships three times. On this occasion he said, "Although I have deeply felt China's great progress and development each time I visit, so many advanced warships and vessels still exceeds my expectations. Fully equipped, a gallant array and strict discipline—all of these embody the image of the Chinese Navy as a responsible and mighty naval force."

The Brazilian Navy commander, Admiral Mora, said, "The transparency and modernization levels of the Chinese Navy are surprising. What I have seen is a real China, a real Chinese Navy."

MULTINATIONAL SAMPAN MATCH

On April 21, 2009, spring filled the air and a sea breeze wafted gently at the Qingdao Olympic Sailing Center. Navy personnel from 13 countries, including Brazil, Pakistan, India and New Zealand, looked forward to the upcoming major sporting event with cheer and laughter. The Multinational Sampan Match in celebration of the sixtieth anniversary of the founding of the PLAN was about to begin.

Shortly after 8:00 a.m., 500 or so residents of Qingdao waited expectantly at the Sailing Center for the match to start. One excited young man told a reporter, "I really look forward to this match between the Chinese Navy and the navies of other countries!"

Soon, the contestants themselves were arriving at the Center. These weren't professional athletes but rather the officers and men off the warships that had come to join in the PLAN founding anniversary celebration. On the two Chinese teams were young sailors from China's nuclear-powered submarine #406 and guided-missile destroyer #116.

At the staging area, the contestants weren't feeling at all tense about the impending mega-games. Everybody wore a happy smile. Although they spoke different languages, the young sailors from the different countries greeted and waved to each other to sprightly welcome music. They took photos for each other. In such a friendly atmosphere, the match wasn't so much like a sports tournament as the start of a grand gathering. A laughing young woman from New Zealand, a vice captain, told nearby reporters, "I'm an amateur. I'll participate in the match as a helmsman. Hope my team won't be last!"

The match began. The men on China's warship 116, in white uniforms, lined up on deck to watch.

When the starting gun was fired, the contestants on the first team started to row. The white sampans kept close to the surface of the water and gradually sailed into the distance to the sound of a sports song as seven white gulls flew low over the water. With the sampans sailing in the distance, a director in charge of electronics and communications commented, "The sampan race is the competitive sport that most embodies team spirit. People make a concerted effort to move fast! The competition today is a wonderful bridge for naval forces around the world to build friendships."

Shortly afterward, the competing sampans returned. The team from submarine 406 was seriously in the lead and reached the finish line by an overwhelming margin. Second and third places were taken by India and New Zealand, respectively.

The awards ceremony was fabulous and bustling. The competing sailors were neither complacent at winning nor disgruntled at losing. They all sang and danced in front of the winner's platform, and their faces radiated joy, from the top three winners to those who got simply a "Friendship Award." They waved their national flags and held bouquets and trophies high. They hugged as they waited for cameras to record the memorable moment. One Pakistan Navy officer said, "This was my first time coming to China. I deeply feel the kindness and enthusiasm of the Chinese people. Today, I am moved even more by such a big event. This truly is an international celebration of friendship!"

THE GRAND MARITIME PARADE

April 23, 2009, marked an important day in the progress of the Chinese Navy. It was the first time China hosted a multinational maritime parade, the largest maritime parade in which the People's Navy had participated. This parade took place on the Yellow Sea near Qingdao. China's President and Chairman of the Military Commission of the CCCPC, Hu Jintao, and senior domestic and foreign naval officers boarded the guided-missile destroyer *Shijiazhuang* to review the warships on parade.

At 2:20 p.m., the officers and men marched past. Immediately, the long column of the Chinese warship formation, stretching as far as the eye could see and comprising 25 submarines, destroyers, frigates and guided-missile destroyers, began moving past the reviewing ship as thousands of officers and men lined up on deck.

The first vessel to be inspected was the nuclear-powered submarine *Great Wall 6*, and this parade was its public debut. Behind it sailed the nuclear-powered *Great Wall 3* and the conventionally powered *Great Wall 218* and *177*.

Behind the submarines, the destroyer formation, comprised of five guided-missile destroyers including the *Shenyang*, and the frigate formation, seven ships including the *Zhoushan*, and the dock landing *Kunlunshan* (carrying 260 marines) passed in review.

While the surface warships were in review, early warning and electronic intelligence aircraft roared into the sky. The China-designed and made fighter-bombers and latest model fighters flew for review in two formations. Following these were antisubmarine and casualty helicopters.

Behind the destroyer and frigate formations, eight latest model stealth missile ships, camouflage-painted the color of the ocean, passed the *Shijiazhuang* at full speed, like swift arrows.

At 2:42, the parade review was concluded, and this signaled the beginning of the maritime review.

The 21 foreign warships that had crossed the sea to attend the celebration anchored in a long row from west to east, in this order: combat ships, landing ships, auxiliary ships, training ships. The ships were decorated with flags, following the custom of naval forces around the world. The visiting sailors were lined up on deck. Nearly half the warships had come to China before, like the French missile frigate *Vendemiaire*, which had visited seven times, and some warships that had been involved in joint military exercises with the Chinese Navy.

The *Shijiazhuang* sailed slowly forward now, with Chairman Hu Jintao onboard still, for a review of the foreign vessels.

8. THE COURSE OF FRIENDSHIP

Hu Jintao waving a greeting

Sailing behind the Chinese guided-missile destroyer *Xi'ning*, the missile destroyer *Varyag*, the flagship of the Russian Pacific Fleet, was the first to be reviewed; next came the U.S guided-missile destroyer *Fitzgerald*, the Indian guided-missile destroyers INS *Mumbai* and INS *Ranveer*, the South Korean KDX-II amphibious assault ship *Dokdo* and missile destroyer *Kang Gam Chan*, the Pakistani missile destroyer PNS *Bardar* and supply ship *Nasser*, the Bengal missile frigate *Osman*, the French missile frigate *Vendemiaire*, the Thai missile frigates HTMS *Bangpakong* and *Taksin*, New Zealand's missile frigate *Te Mana* and supply ship *Endeavour*, the Singaporean missile frigate *Formidable*, the Australian patrol boat *Pirie* and supply ship *Success*, the Brazilian amphibious landing ship *Garcia D'Avila*, the Canadian comprehensive depot ship *Protecteur* and the Russian auxiliary ship *Salome*. The last to be reviewed was the Mexican sail training vessel, *Cuauhtémoc*. Gathered there on the blue sea, these ships made for a spectacular picture.

Each time the *Shijiazhuang* passed, the warships' watch officers' whistles sounded. The officers raised their hands in greeting, and the passing sailors saluted. The *Shijiazhuang* whistled in return. Chairman

Hu Jintao and the heads of the other nations' delegations waved to the officers and men on the ships being reviewed. Reporters from each country took photos, recording the significant moment as the Chinese Navy held its first international maritime parade.

At 3:03 p.m., the grand Yellow Sea Military Review concluded. As the whistles of the warships sounded, startled gulls flew up from the sea.

HARMONIOUS OCEAN ENVIRONMENT

China celebrated the sixtieth anniversary of the PLAN by way of exchanges among multinational naval forces. The theme, "Harmonious Ocean Environment," embodied the hope China holds to strengthen its communications and cooperation with naval forces around the world, to enhance mutual understanding and to develop a harmonious ocean environment.

Today, the oceans, which cover 70 percent of the Earth, aren't peaceful. Pirate activity is rampant off the coast of Somalia. Natural disasters like tsunamis claim countless lives now and then. The organized crime rate for such things as maritime drug trafficking, human smuggling and human trafficking goes up every year. Such problems pose grave threats to local sea areas and have become the single biggest obstacle for countries around the world seeking to build a long-term, stable and prosperous marine environment.

A harmonious world cannot exist without peaceful oceans. And to achieve peaceful oceans, it is imperative that naval forces communicate and cooperate.

Commander Wu Shengli has urged the world on behalf of the Chinese Navy that naval forces should work together to promote mutual trust, according to applicable U.N. agreements and conventions; should insist on resolving sea disputes by equitable negotiation; and should seek out common interests.

In nearly two days of response, high-level naval officers from around the world reacted positively to this initiative. They agree that our blue planet will never be a harmonious world without harmonious blue seas.

8. THE COURSE OF FRIENDSHIP

High-level dialogue

According to the U.S. Navy chief of Naval Operations, Gary Roughead, if we always dealt with maritime disputes through cooperation, we would be embracing a more harmonious world. And a healthy cooperation and relationship, marked by mutual trust between the Chinese and U.S. navies, will present new opportunities for the two nations to improve overall relations.

Roughead added that he believed the Combined Task Force 151, sent by the U.S. Navy to Somali waters, and the warship formations dispatched by the Chinese for convoy task work around the area are an example of highly effective cooperation. But, he said, there's still a lot of room for the two nations' navies to cooperate more in international humanitarian assistance and joint maritime search and rescue.

The French naval commander for the Pacific said that China's celebration of the sixtieth anniversary of the founding of its Navy afforded a new platform for the world's navies to promote information communications and mutual trust. He expressed the hope that this China-sponsored multinational activity would mark the beginning of a new international multilateral military exchange mechanism. He said it was his opinion that in the twenty-first century no one country can fight alone against the various security threats at sea. He added that in the second half of the twentieth century many countries adhered to the Five Principles of Peaceful Coexistence put forward by former premier Zhou Enlai and achieved remarkable results in maritime security.

Basically, admirals of different races and beliefs spoke as one: "The oceans need harmony, and the world's naval forces should cooperate!"

The Chinese Navy will continue to commit to promoting communication, understanding and cooperation between the navies of the world in accordance with the theme of harmonious oceans and so will play an active and constructive role in promoting mutual development.

BIBLIOGRAPHY

Books

Huang Dosheng, *China's Spirit in the South China Sea*, Guangzhou: Guangdong Renmin Publishing Press, 1996.

Xu Ge, *Defending Coastal Areas and Territorial Seas with Powerful Anchors*, Beijing: Hai Chao Publishing House, 1999.

Cao Baojian & Guo Fuwen, *Contemplations about the Pacific Ocean*, Beijing: National Defense University Press, 1989.

Su Shiliang, *Naval Weapons*, Beijing: China Children's Press & Publication Group, 2002.

Lu Qiming, *The Founding Fathers of the First People's Navy*, Beijing: Hai Chao Publishing House, 2006.

Huang Yanping, *Glorious Sailing*, Beijing: Hai Chao Publishing House, 2001.

Editorial Committee of the series on the History of the People's Liberation Army, ed., *Naval History*, Beijing: Chinese People's Liberation Army Publishing House, 1989.

Editorial Board of the series on Modern China, ed., *Modern Chinese Navy*, Beijing: China Social Sciences Publishing House, 1987.10.

Qiming Lu, *The Pride of the Sea*, Beijing: Ocean Press, 1983.

Editorial Committee of the Dictionary of the Navy, ed., *The Dictionary of the Navy*, Shanghai: Shanghai Lexicographic Publishing House, 1993.

Yong Kang, *The Heroic Yijiangshan Islands Landing Operation*, Jinan: Huang He Publishing Company, 2008.

Tie Liu, *The Chinese Naval Destroyers*, Beijing: Chinese People's Liberation Army Publishing House, 2002.

Zheng Huaisheng, *Dispatching Troops to Fight Floods in 1998*, Beijing: Modern China Publishing House, 1998.

Shi Diansheng, *An Outline of the History of the Chinese Navy*, Beijing: Hai Chao Publishing House, 2006.

Han Yu, *Submarines*, Beijing: People's Publishing House, 1996.

Tang Zhiba, *Submarine Chasers*, Beijing: People's Publishing House, 1996.

Zhang Xu & Fan Xiaoyan, *Military Speedboats*, Beijing: People's Publishing House, 1996.

Li Jie et al., *Mine Warfare Ships*, Beijing: People's Publishing House, 1996.7.

Xu Ming, *Veritable Records of Modern Weapons*, Beijing: Aviation Industry Press, 2009.

Liu Huaqing, *Liu Huaqing's Memoirs*, Beijing: Chinese People's Liberation Army Publishing House, 2004.

Li Jie & Wei Dong, *General Stars in Naval Battles*, Guangzhou: Guangdong Economic Press, 2011.

Liu Daosheng, *Liu Daosheng's Memoirs*, Beijing: Hai Chao Publishing House, 1992.

Ye Fei, *Ye Fei's Memoirs*, Beijing: Chinese People's Liberation Army Publishing House, 2007.

Hu Xueqing & Sun Guo, *Senior General Xiao Jingguang*, Beijing: Chinese People's Liberation Army Literature and Art Publishing House, 1998.

Hu Xueqing & Sun Guo, *Xiao Jingguang: the Senior General*, Beijing: People's Liberation Army Literature and Art Publishing House, 2007.

Hu Shihong, *The Military Life of Zhang Aiping, one of the Founding Generals of the People's Navy*, Beijing: People's Publishing House, 1996.

You Lan et al., ed., *Remembering Zhang Aiping*, Beijing: Chinese People's Liberation Army Publishing House, 2004.

Zhang Sheng, *Coming from the Wars: Dialogues between the Military Men of Two Generations—A Record of Zhang Aiping's Life*, Beijing: China Youth Publishing House, 2008.

Chang Da, *Reminiscences of the Experiences in the Battle of the Paracel Islands*, Beijing: Hua Ling Publishing House, 2004.

Zhang Wenmu, *On Chinese Maritime Power*, Beijing: Ocean Press, 2009.

Xiao Jiangguang, *Xiao Jingguang's Memoirs (sequel)*, Beijing: Chinese People's Liberation Army Publishing House, 1989.

Xu Xuezeng, *The Blue Battlefields*, Beijing: Military Science Publishing House, 1995.

Yang Xiaojing, *The People's Republic Embracing the Coasts*, Beijing: Chinese Navy Press, 1989.

Hu Yanlin et al., *Inspiring Awe through Coastal Areas and Territorial Seas: Record of Actual Events*, Beijing: National Defense University Press, 1996.

Wang Peiyun, *Roaring Waves throughout the China Sea*, Beijing: Writers Publishing House, 2010.

Wang Yan, *Wow! The Sixth Fleet*, Beijing: Hai Chao Publishing House, 1995.

Journals

The Modern Navy by the Political Department of the Navy

Military History Review by the China People's Revolution Military Museum

Military History by the Academy of Military Science of the Chinese PLA

Military Historical Research by Shanghai Brach College of Nanjing Political College

Weapons by the National Weapons Science Research Academy *Ordnance Industry Science Technology* by the Shaanxi Science History Association

Modern Ships by the China Ship Information Center

Naval and Merchant Ships by the Chinese Society of Naval Architecture and Marine Engineering